Coupling

i have yearned and i have learned. yet there is more to see on this coaster of romantic love. i seek its highs and brace for its slows.

Samuel Field

This is a work of personal expression,

it reflects the authors feelings and

may not reflect others perspective and intent

First published 2018 by YndFwd

www.yndfwd.com

Cataloguing-in-Publication entry is available
from the National Library of Australia
http://catalogue.nla.gov.au

Gratitude

This journey of putting old feelings into something shareable has intrinsically involved the support of many friends in different ways. While not a full list of friends who supported, some especially stood alongside with helpful acts and encouragement when it was needed.

Azzelarabe Taleb-Bendiab (support)
Jacqui Taleb-Bendiab (drilling my english)
Rob Martin (support, photographic advice)
Murray Jongeling (layout & encourgement)
Lynn MacMillan (loud encourgement)
Dave Stephens (clear encourgement)
Deepti Heera (strong encourgement)

everyone's story
uniquely their own
reflections in others
bring us home

Contents

Yearning

let me reach you
wordless, soundless
one hand stretched forth
its partner found
my fingers on yours
our eyes, betraying thoughts
connection, beyond time

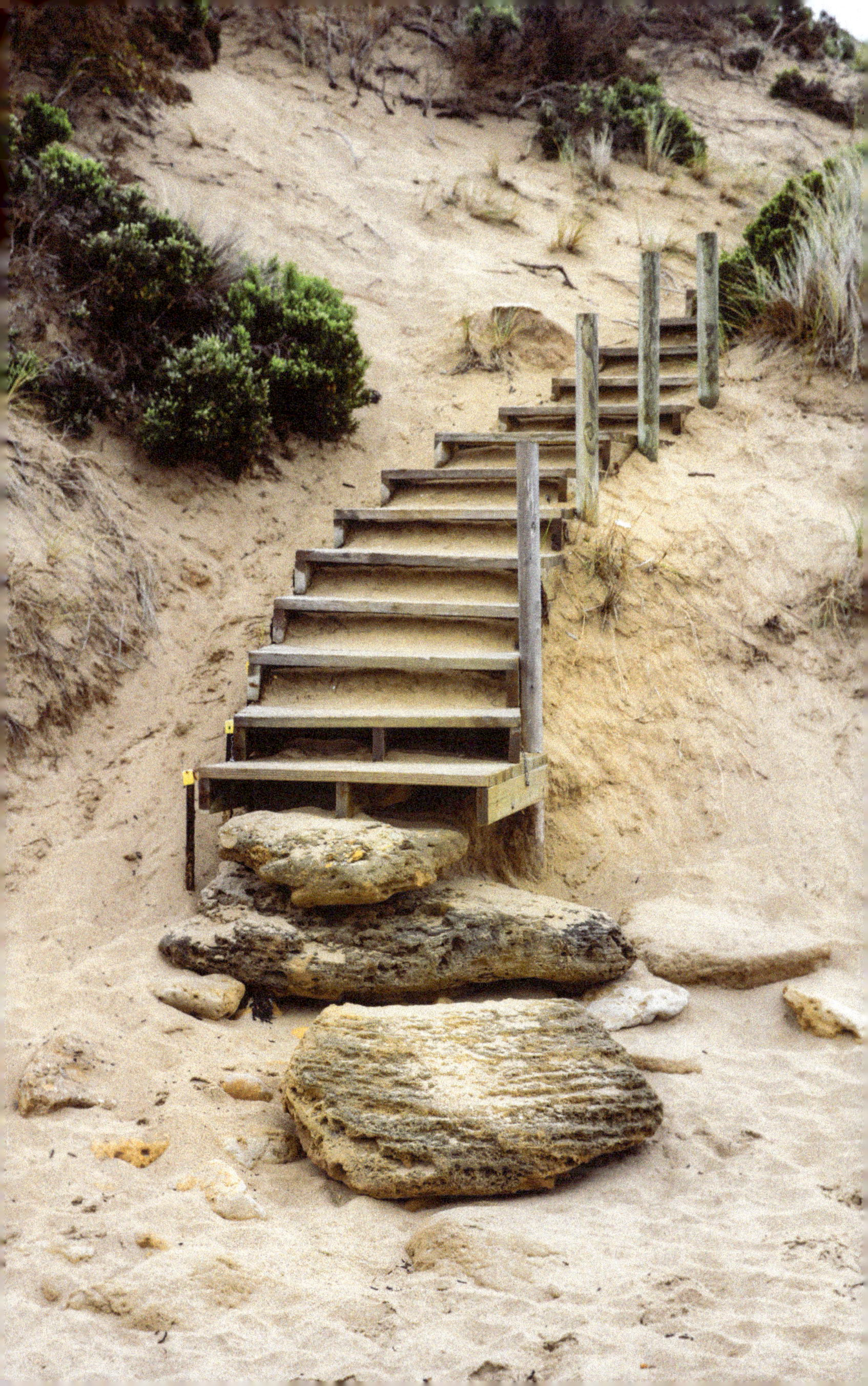

my heart is broad and deep
like a sea tossed and spurned
its love sees no horizon
its depth's unplumbed
its one desire, beholden
to the clearest vision of you

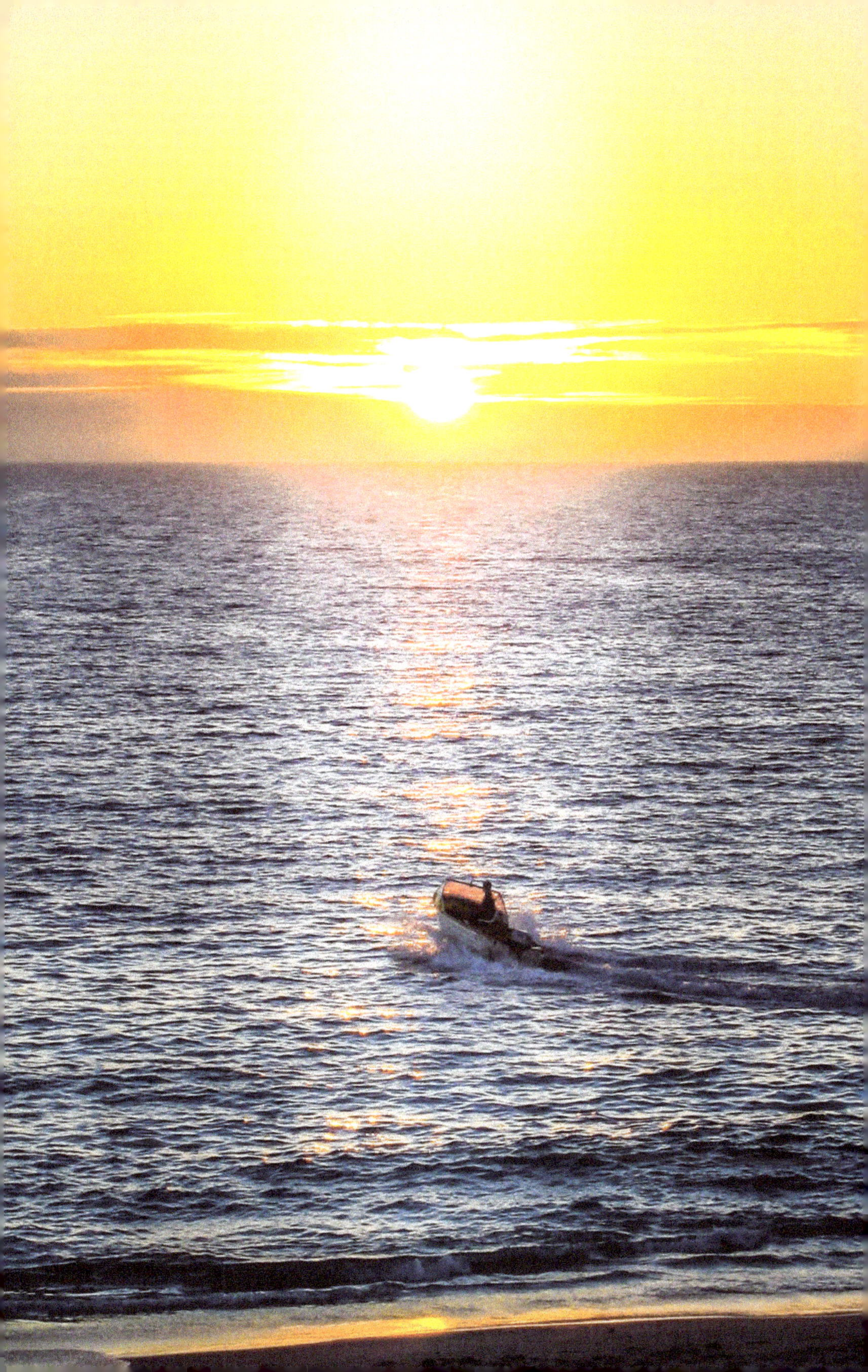

everybody dreams
some asleep
some awake
no matter
how i dream, or why
i know
i dream of you
i dream of being at your side

i see the water
i feel the stream
i watch leaves
moving in trees

in the distance i look
you're standing there
with no disguise

my heart pounds, legs stride
my will takes me
love draws me
to your side

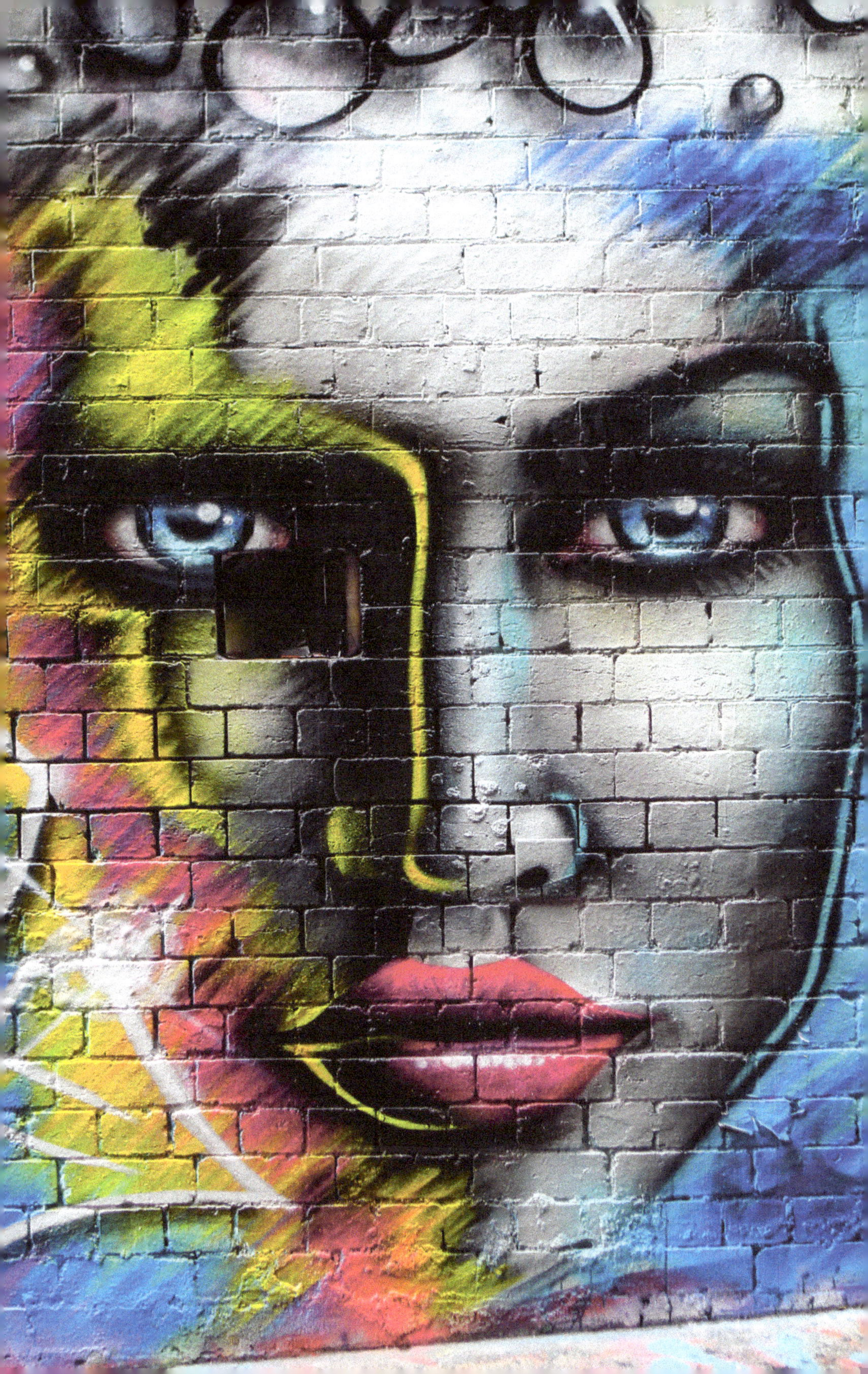

Cleaving

i want you close
our minds known
plunging to depths
journey unknown

sailing a new ocean's wind
riding it's gentle breeze
deeper we are called
together

stand on the precipice
face desert plains
holding hands, call this ours
shared, never alone

pause the tape on rush
settle, hold our own
pause for breath
drink of life again,
love, passion and trust

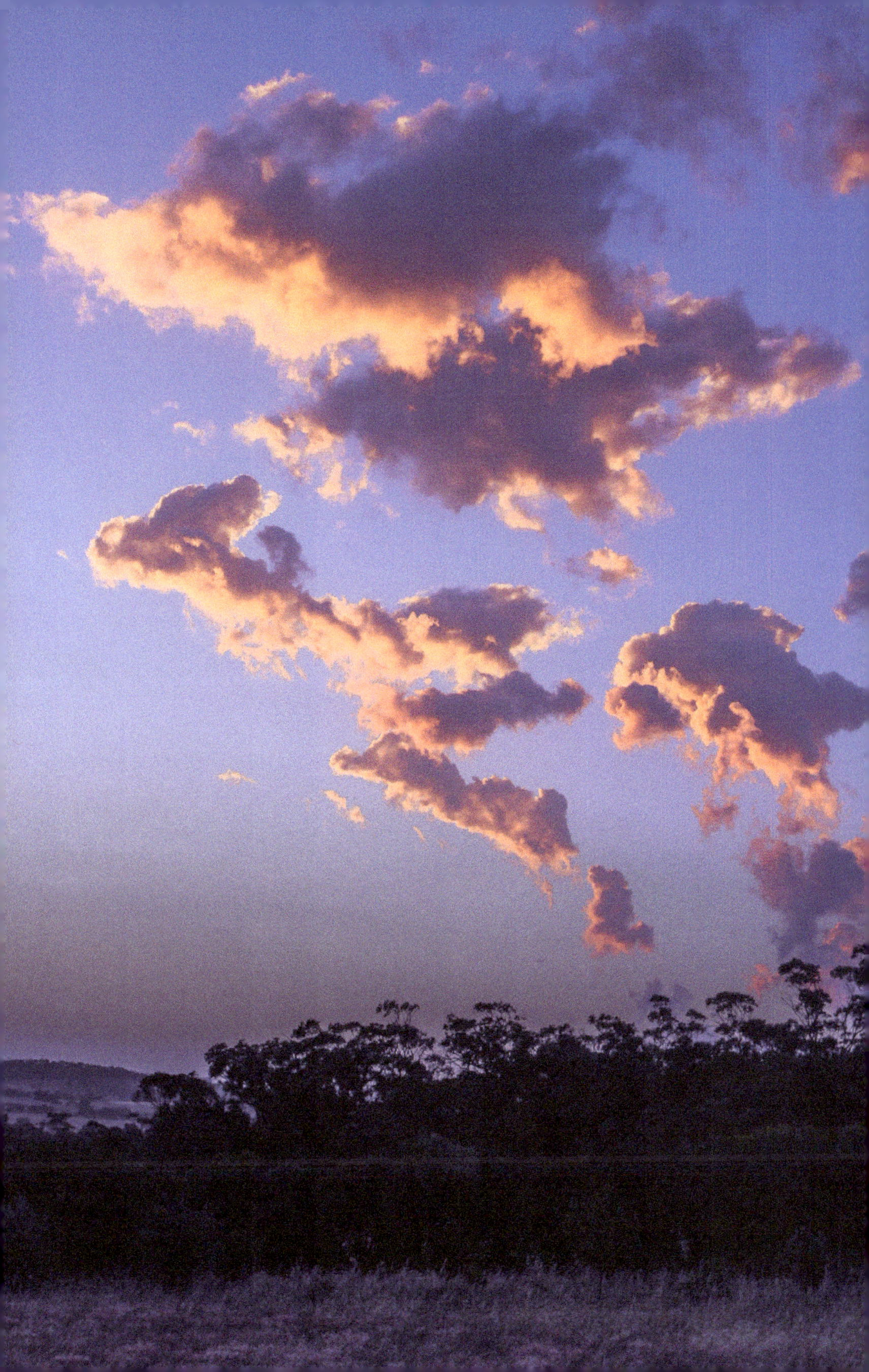

two hearts
two minds
one journey
roads entwined

decisions to share
choices to bind
hearts cleaving
leaving old ways behind

gentle touches
loving kisses
heartfelt hugs
tender reaches

slowly it changes
hearts beat
two become one
a little more each time

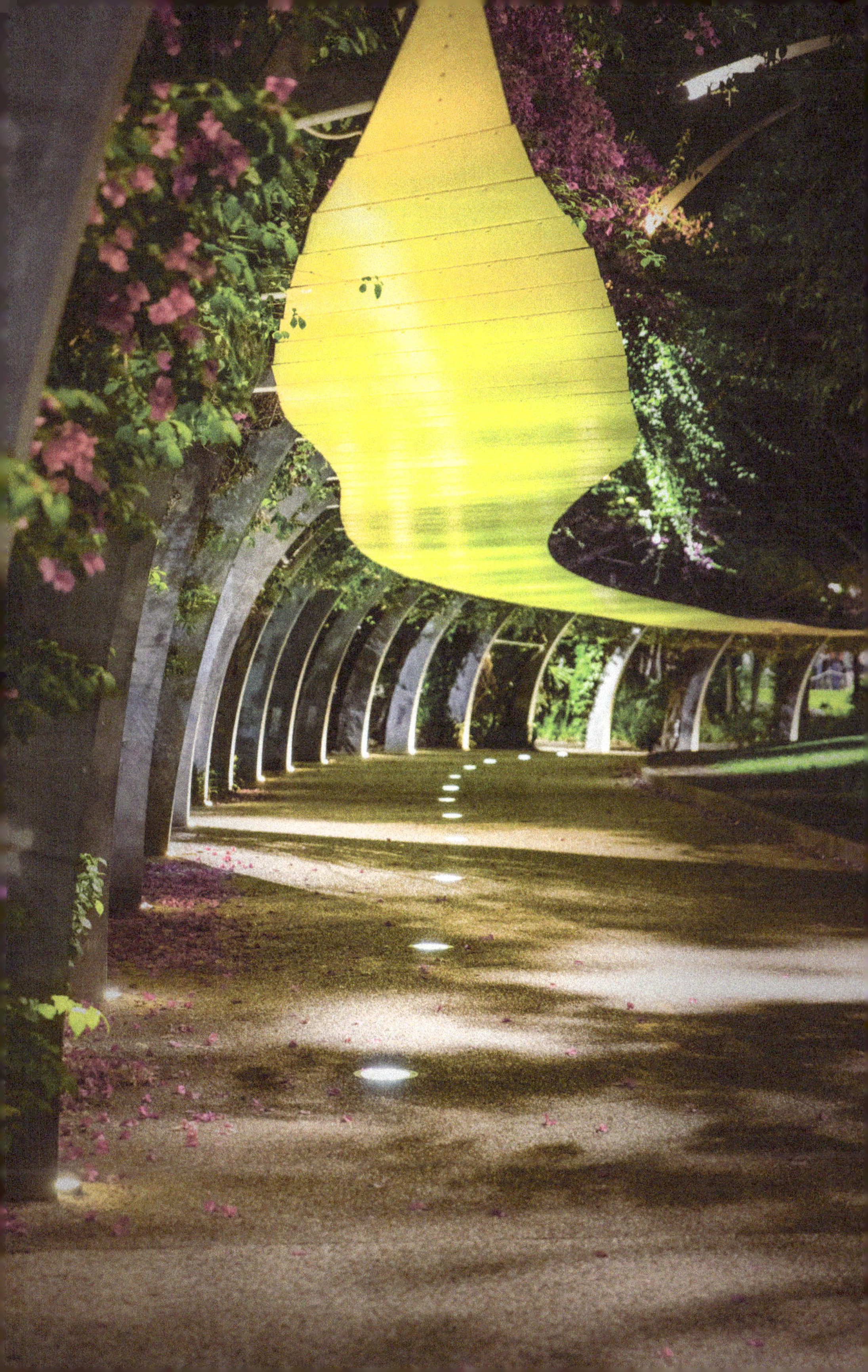

cry freedom
hold to joy
life is no mere ember
quickening comes

joy more than kindled
hope finds its flame
bellows to my strength
hearts fire roars again

beauty, skin and depth
falling under sweet touch
awaken by gentle caress
beating within my chest

my love, my love
your love is mine alone
mine is yours to trust
i'll be with you...always my love

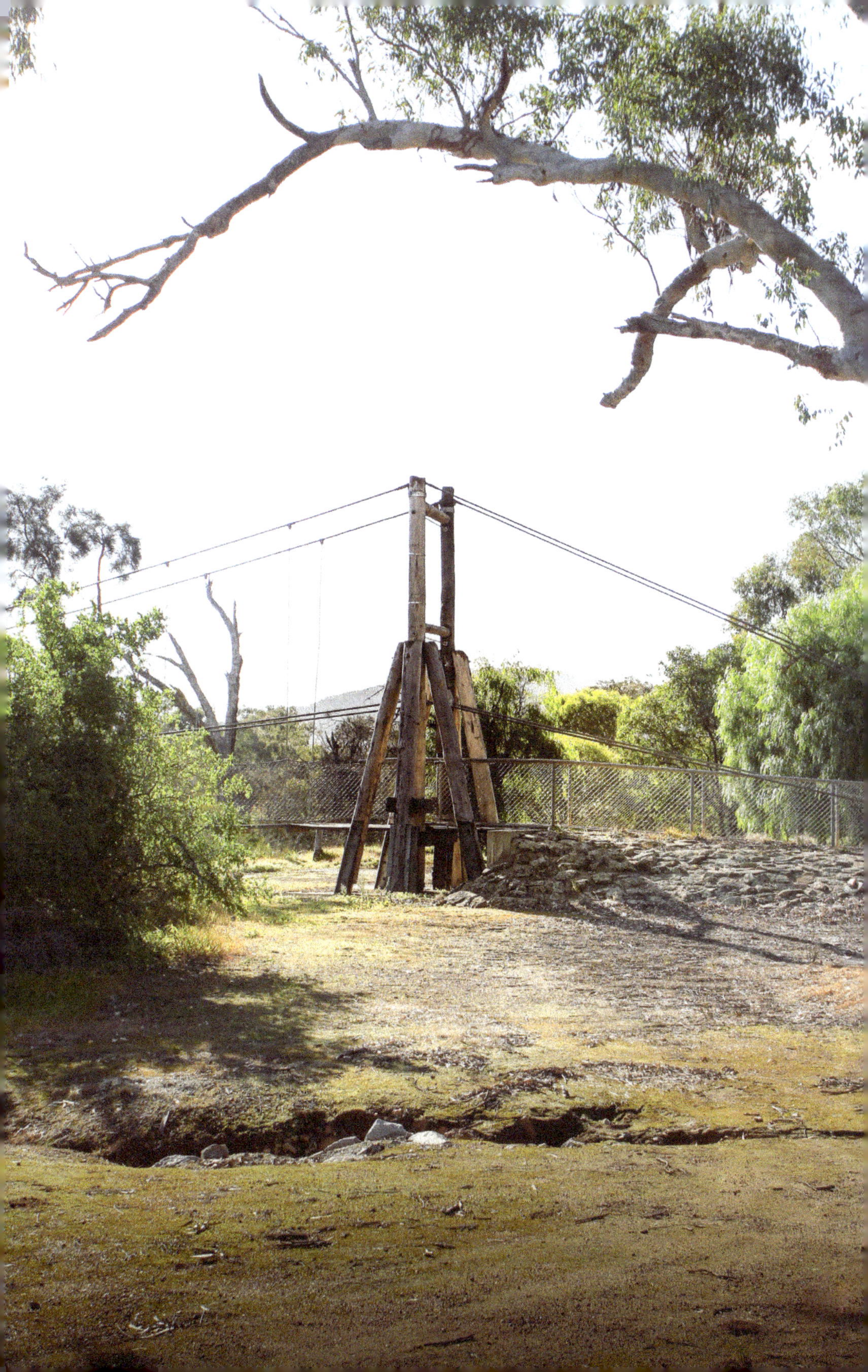

listening ears
my heart hears
words spelt out
messages of your love

when you speak
how you move
love you give
i know your true

gave my heart to you
let you know i'm yours
place your hand in mine
we'll travel side by side

we will see this world
paths never un-entwined
building love deeply
throughout our lives

g-d brought you to me
by grace love grew
i look forward to see
what more he will do

gentle caress
your hand on mine
feel your body
closer to mine

feeling of knowing
pleasure of being
comfort of you
being close to me

Holding

i cry for you
i lie for you
know i'd die for you

hold my heart
touch my skin
take my name
i'll never be the same

your heart is raging
mine is too
your feelings uncontrollable
i feel that way too

your touch is like
chocolate on my tongue
melted, creamy, so dreamy
i want you
i need you

i want to know you
i want to see you
come to me
see me to

lets make love your way
my rules are gone
my heart is open and broad

i know your love
i will share my life
i give to you, all i have
my wife

her eyes were brown
her hair was soft
her clothes were smooth
she just made me sing

i knew her well
she held my heart
whenever i held her hand
i knew we would never part

her eyes were brown
they melted my heart
they picked me up
dropped me straight down

her eyes were brown
twinkled in delight
twinge-d in sadness
whatever the mood
always took me for the ride

i lose myself
and find me again
every time we meet
her eyes were brown

eyes are the window
on the soul so deep
your brown eyes
lead so to you

her eyes were brown
my heart will never escape
it's a prisoner for life
her eyes were brown

close my eyes
i see your face
wind brushes my hand
feel your touch
rain on the bushes
smell your freshness

run a million miles
sleep a thousand nights
drive a hundred k's
think one thought
my minds' possessed
it's by you

since that day
thoughts of you
have followed my every way
the first touch
the first sight
the first smell

have i never seen a woman before?
before i met you, i thought i had!
since you, i'll never see another

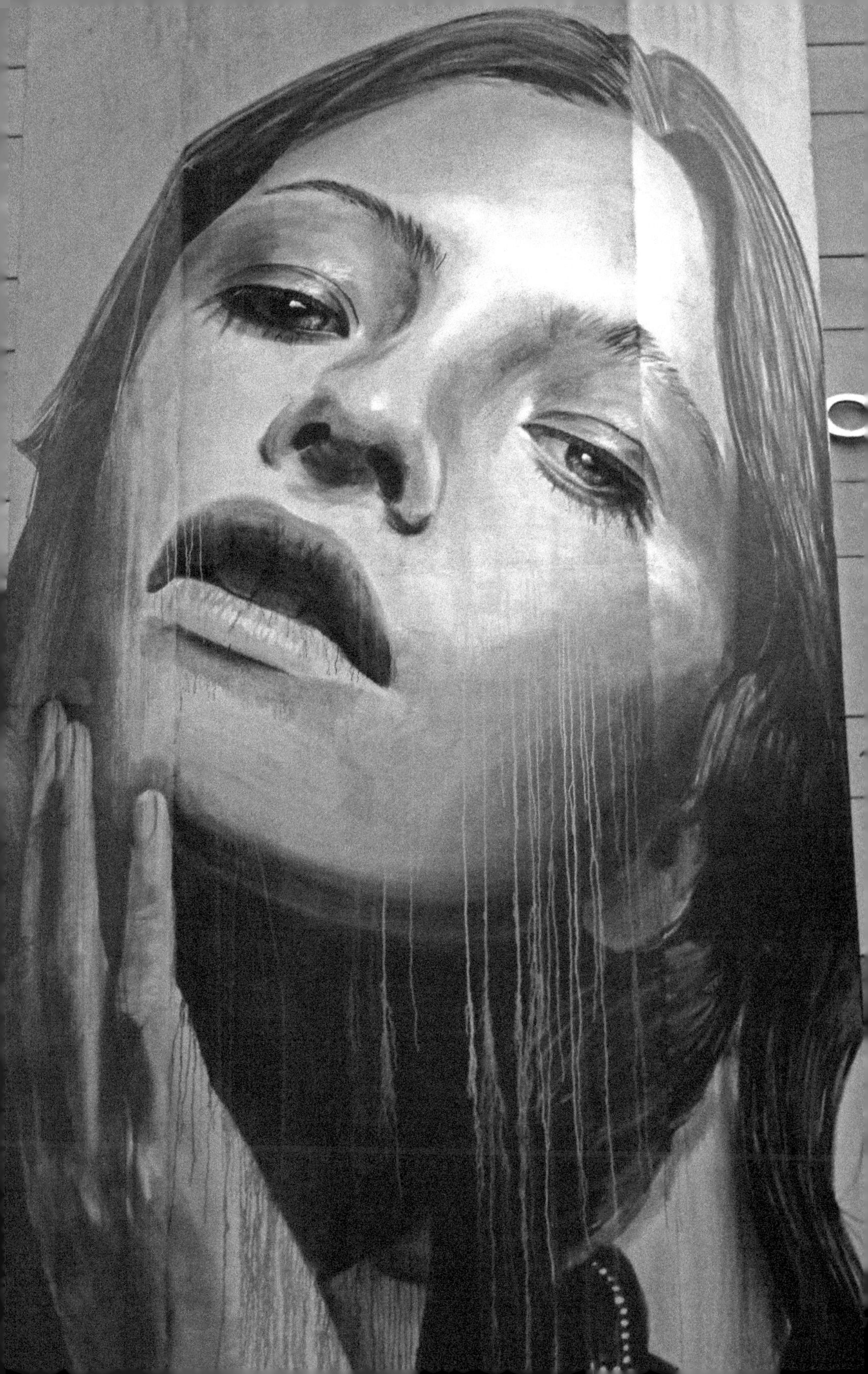

my sweet one
gentle soft skin
heart of gold
breasts so firm
smile so warm

you light up my night
you make me feel alive
thank you for your love
i want to hold you tight
always through the night

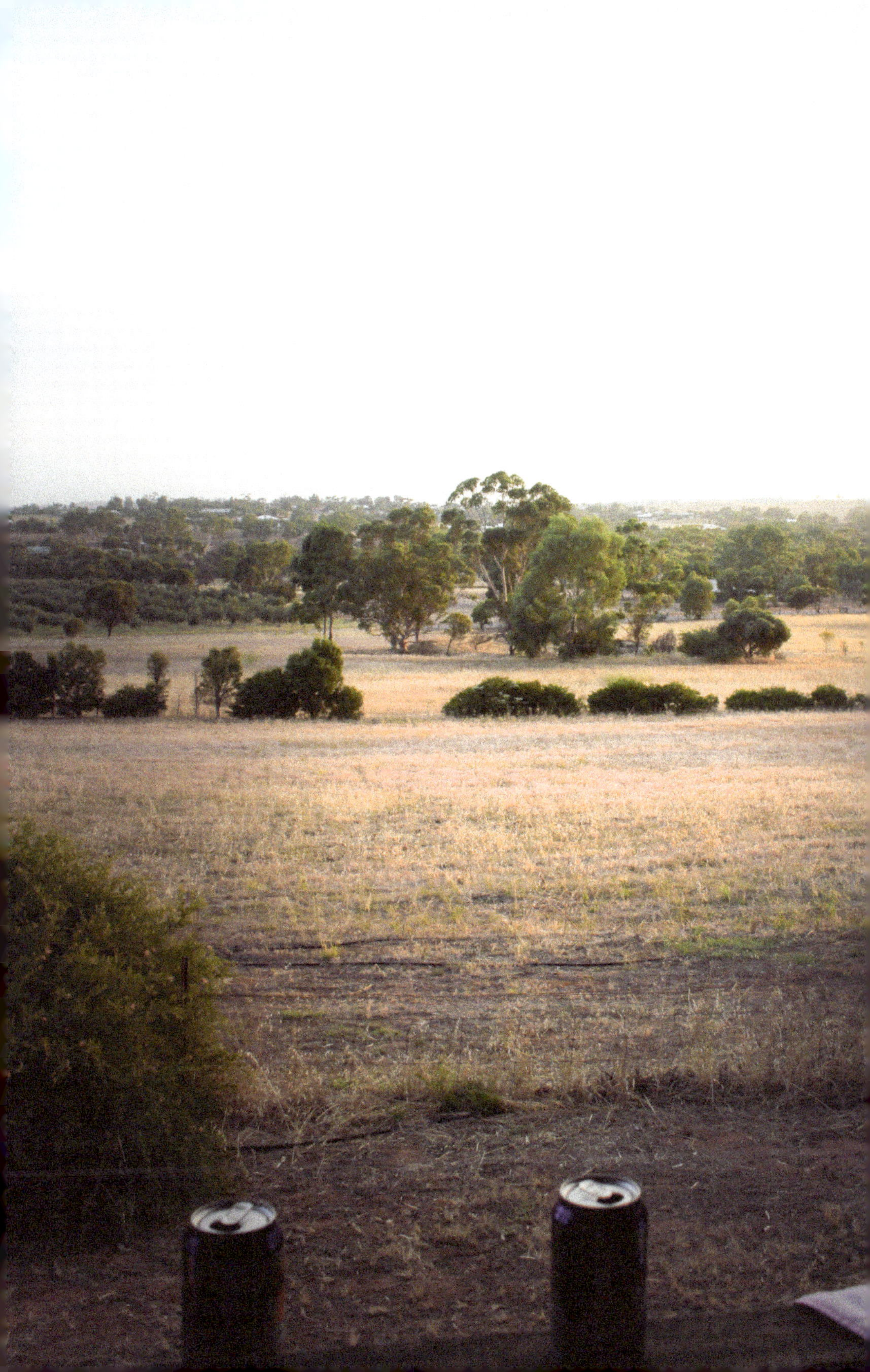

oh my sweet love
heart broken yet strong
a will that holds on
your road was difficult
your burdens not few
i feel lucky i share
the journey with you

you are more beautiful
than you will ever know
believe me when i tell
it's love i will show

i will be there
thick and thin
your heartaches,
your pain i'll share
when you're victorious
know i'll be there

oh my sweet one
i love you, you know
my heart hungers for you
my affections grow
i hope one day you will truly know

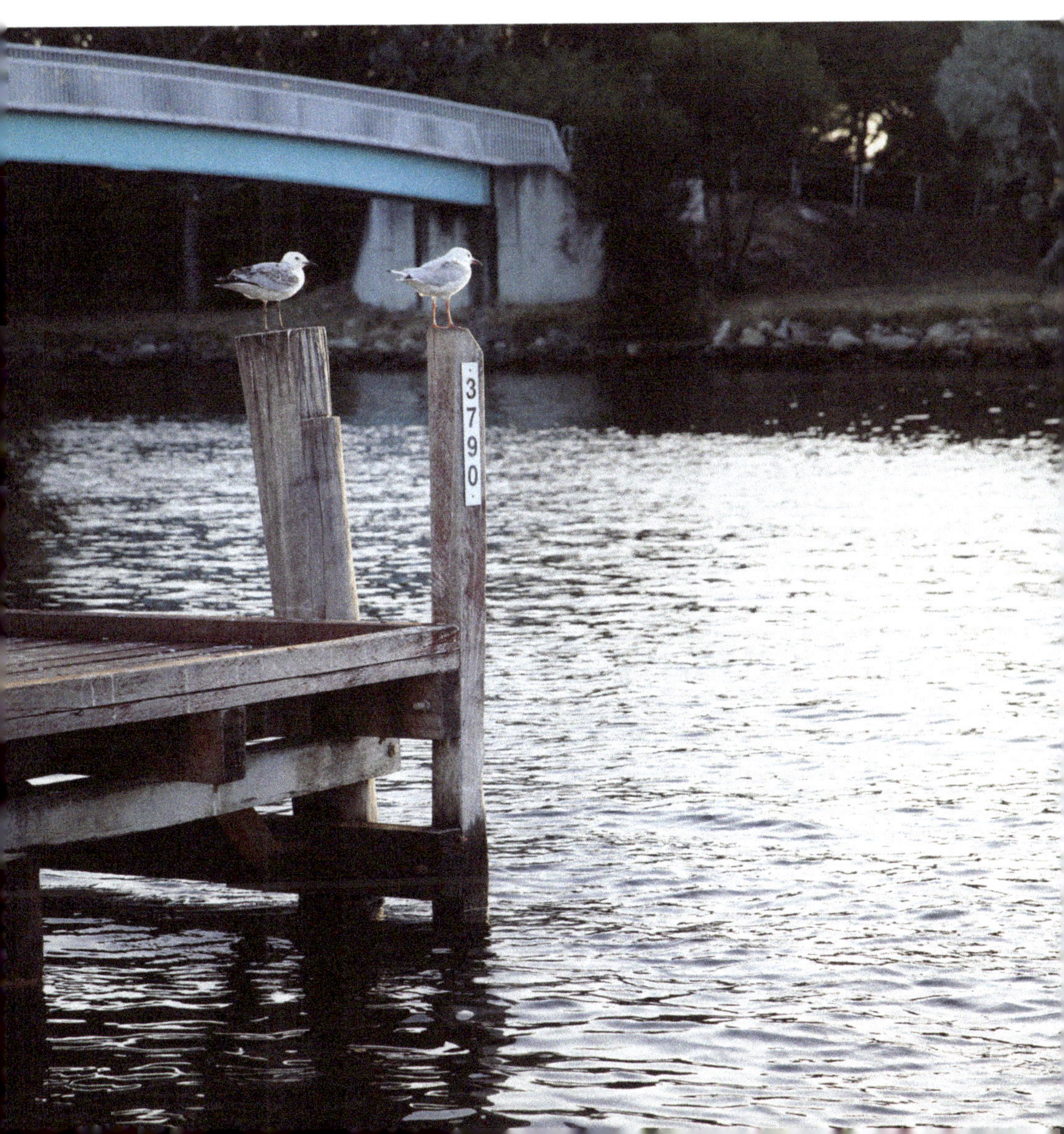

i want to stay that way
to know you
and you know me
just the same

i want to feel your pain
share your joy
to know all
will be okay

it will be
sure as day follows night
sure as life has pain and delight
joy is mine, i've found it

i hold it with your smile
i hold it with your light
i hold it through my nights

i find what i lost
somewhere deep inside
but i saw it first
through your eyes

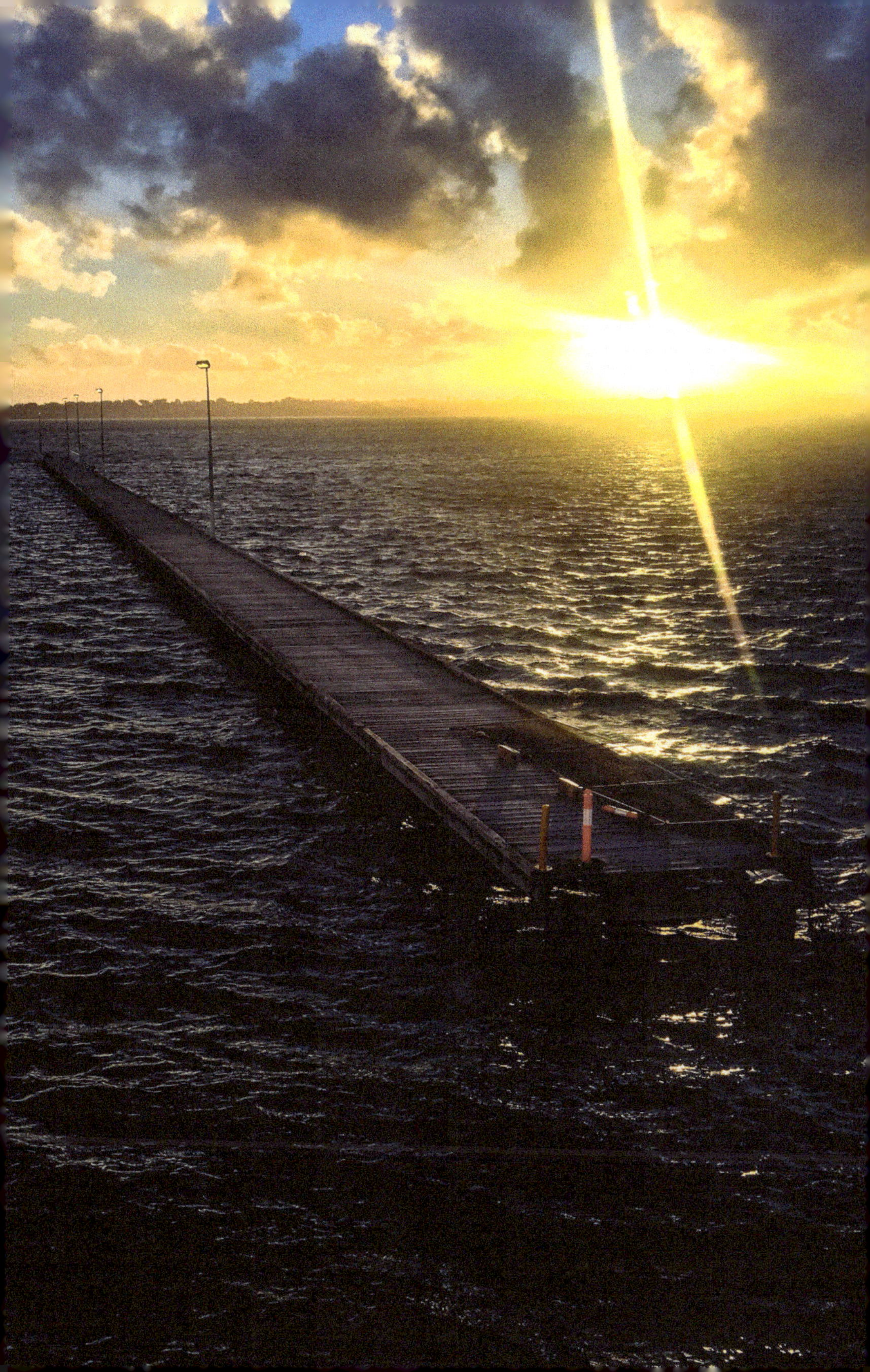

my wife, my wife
joy of my life
woman of my youth
light to my eyes

my bride, my bride
my beautiful bride
with me to spend
the rest of our lives

my wife, my bride
my young and gorgeous pride
i love for people to see her
stand by my side

my wife, my life
i give to her
to trust her with
to love her for
my life, my life

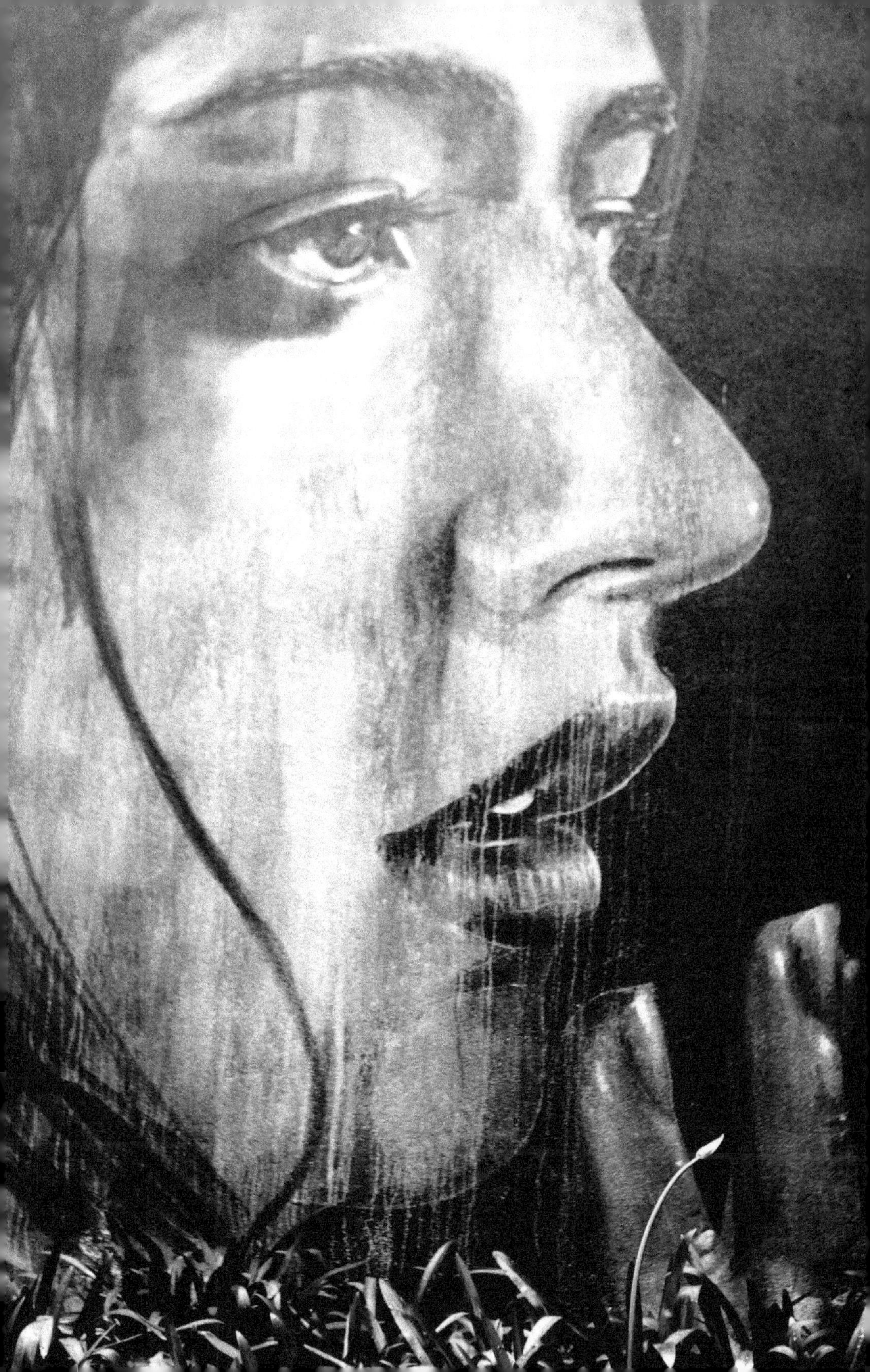

i feel pain ... anger
she smiles and it goes away

little and big things getting to me ... annoyance
she smiles and it goes away

all night getting on my nerves...picking and natt'ing
she smiles and it goes away

i have had enough, about to ... explode
she smiles and it goes away

the next minute, next half hour
she's much nicer, it has all gone away

she drives me mad
she drives me frustrated,
but she smiles
and it all goes away

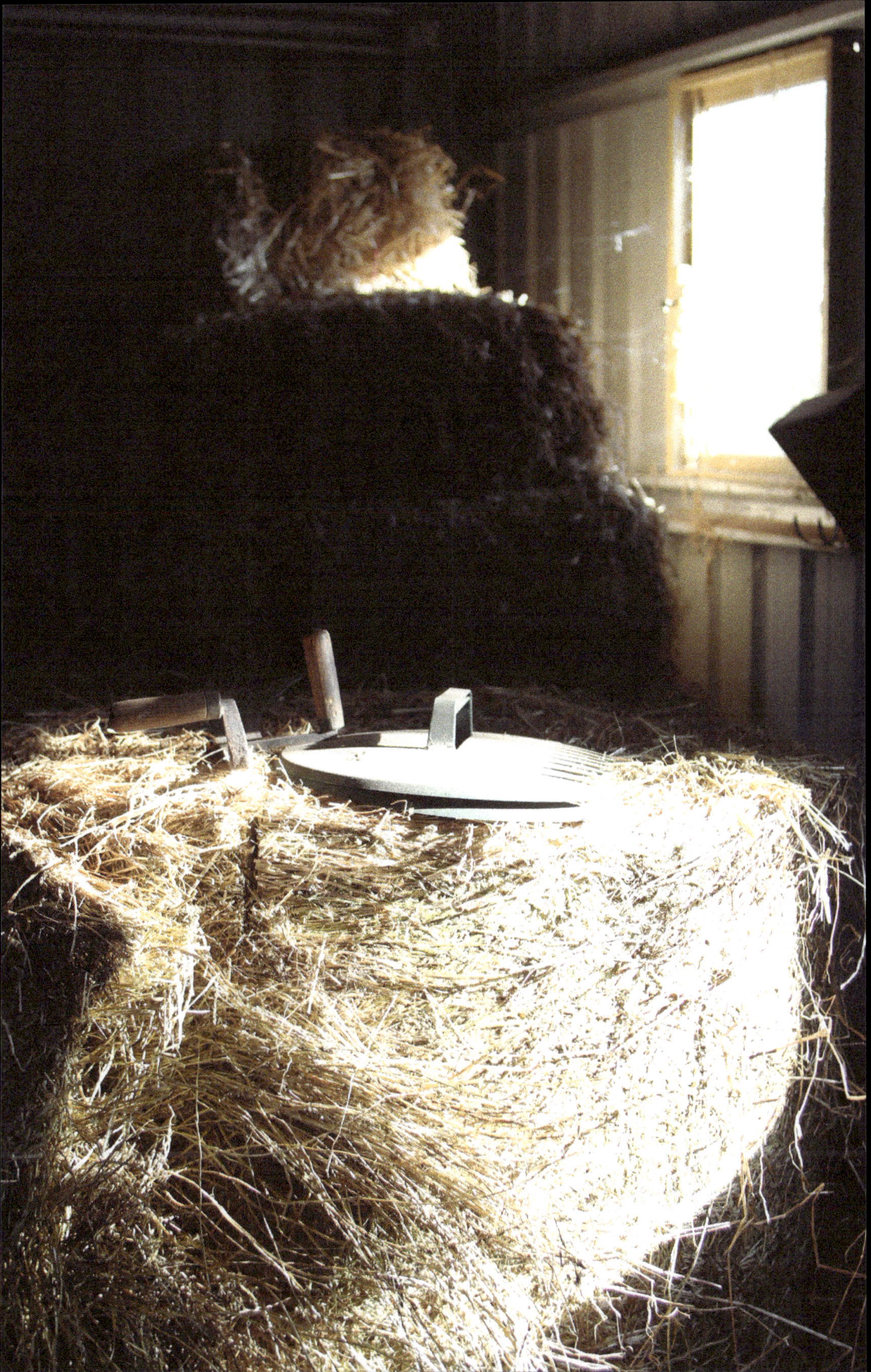

waves thrust, storm bellows
my love holds true and wavers not

rock the boat they call
it's not done they say
push our craft each way

they know not what they do
their ways suck and fail

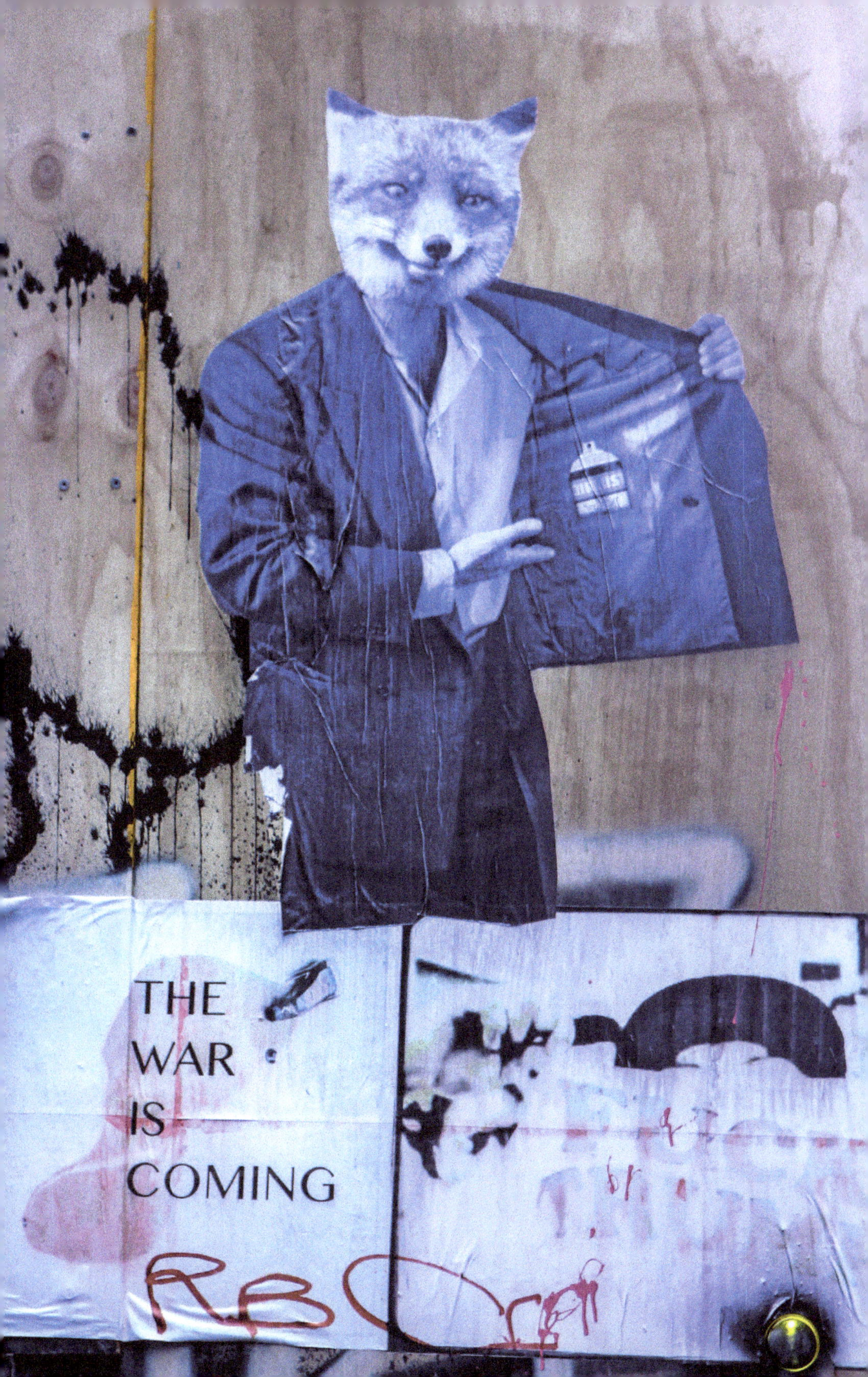
THE
WAR
IS
COMING

Braking

where do i turn
where can i hide
i need to escape
how she leaves me feeling inside

i'm sorry i say
it doesn't make it okay
she loves me no more
or is it just not...more

how do i find
the common thread
the one to bind
the touch of hearts

i want to go out there
talk this through
move on and live
like lovers would

to touch her heart
her touch mine
feel the closeness
with little divide

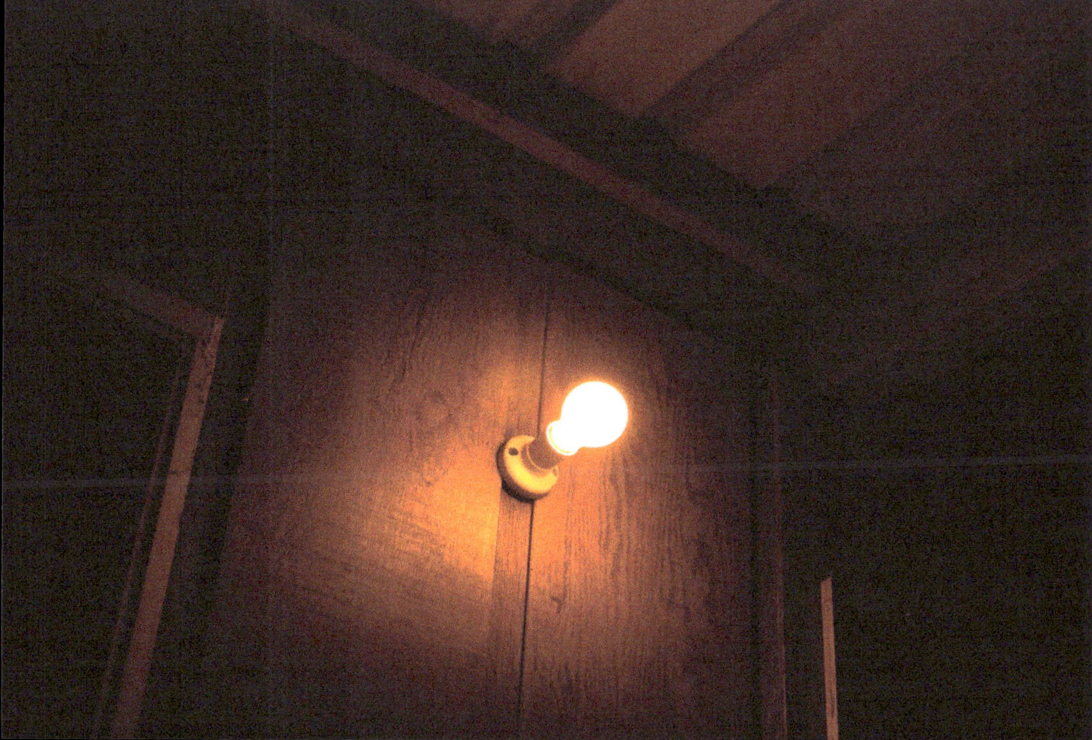

i feel pushed aside
my words shallow, weak
unable to express, to reach you, complete
piercing the parsing mind
what do i mean, what am i saying
what should i change

i want to speak straight
my feeling and thoughts
clarifying as we go
not probing my unconscious mind
i want more signs of warmth
hugs, kisses and encouraging talk

i love you
i know you love me
trust me with your love
its expression is free
no cost, no backlash
it's kind you see

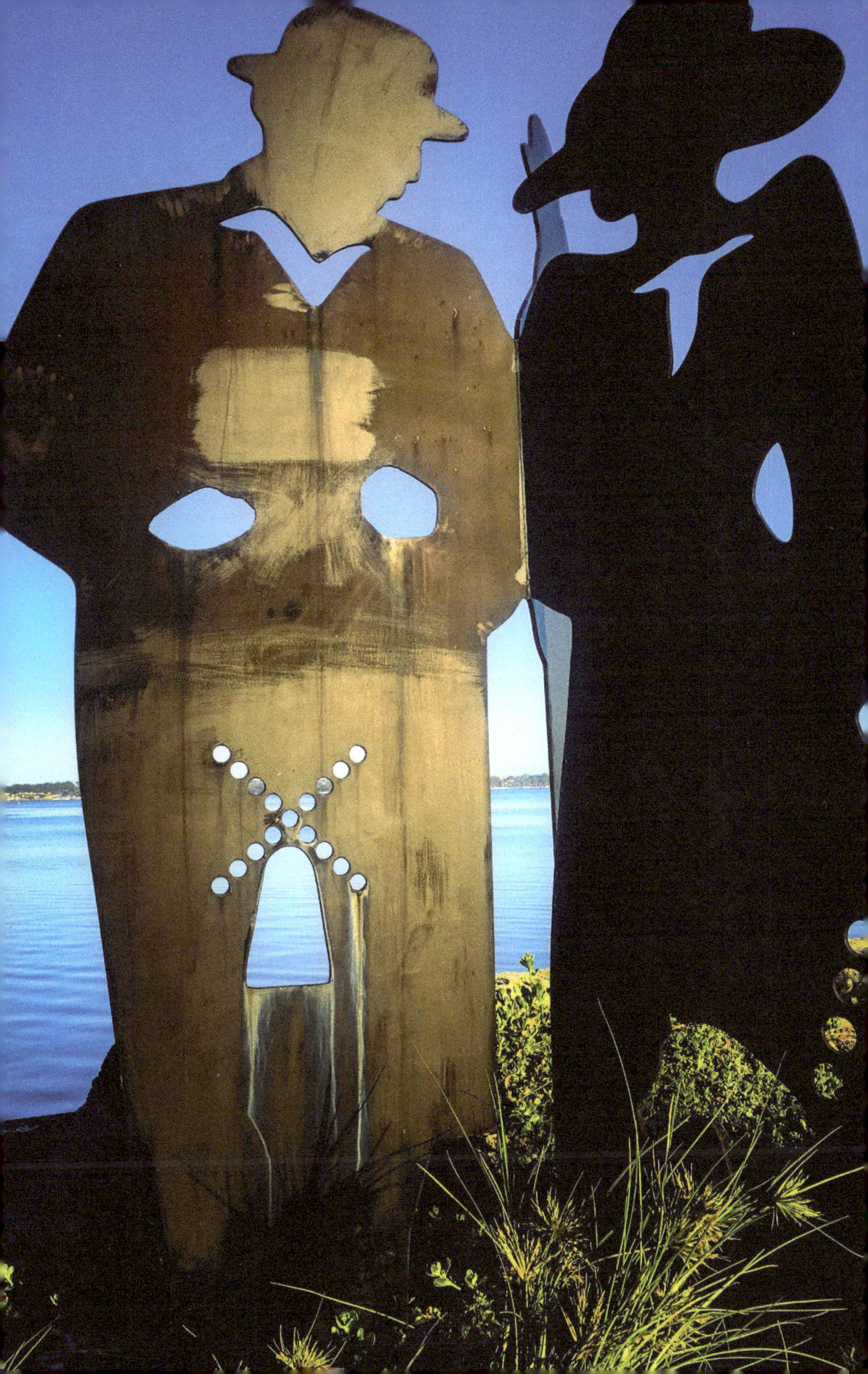

cinnamon and turmeric
her life was spice
words her call
her only door

she let them flow

barb and spite
they cut deep
cut unclean
always cut twice

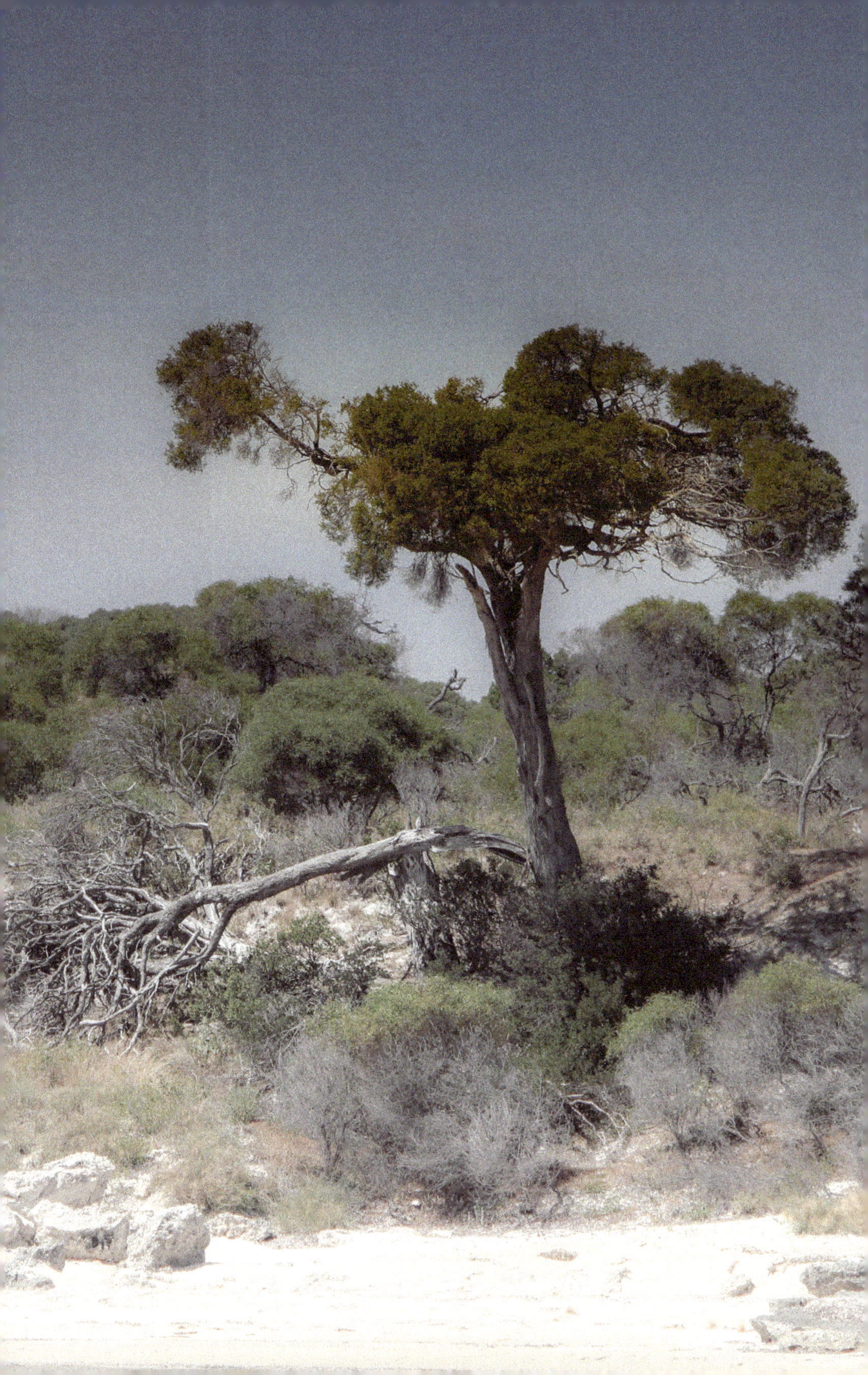

weak, alone
afraid i'm not finding home
my old has gone
an empty shell

promises of love
forming structures of hope
little was added
i was spent waiting

clinging to hope
waiting for the rest
safety, acceptance, affection
promised, not delivered on site

lashing my body to hope
surviving the storm
weak and battered
tired of holding on
to so little, for so long

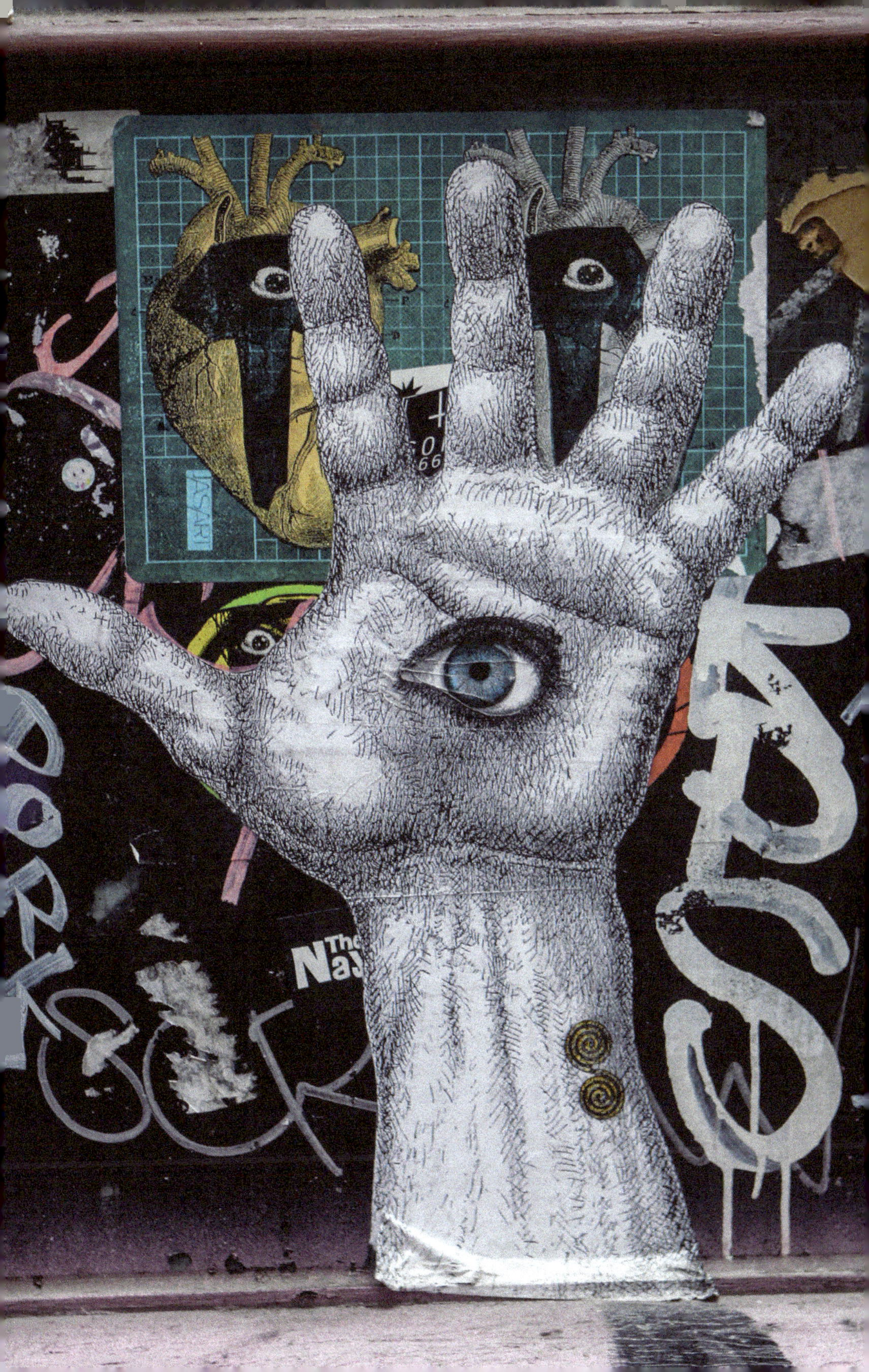

worthless
deeply alone
world goes on without me
my world is not my own

communicate poorly, misjudge my tone
hurting people close to me
people who are my own
feel repulsive, feel my fate

hear voices confirm
fingers of darkness at night
steal my new found home

i am secure, my wife loves me
my friends will stand by me
and my circle respect me

my wife wants me
she yearns my love
she will always love me
more than enough

drained of overcoming power
no rhymes invading my brain
hold fast the line i know to be true
life is now good, much due to you
hold the line and swear it to be true
i'm a decent man and loved as i am

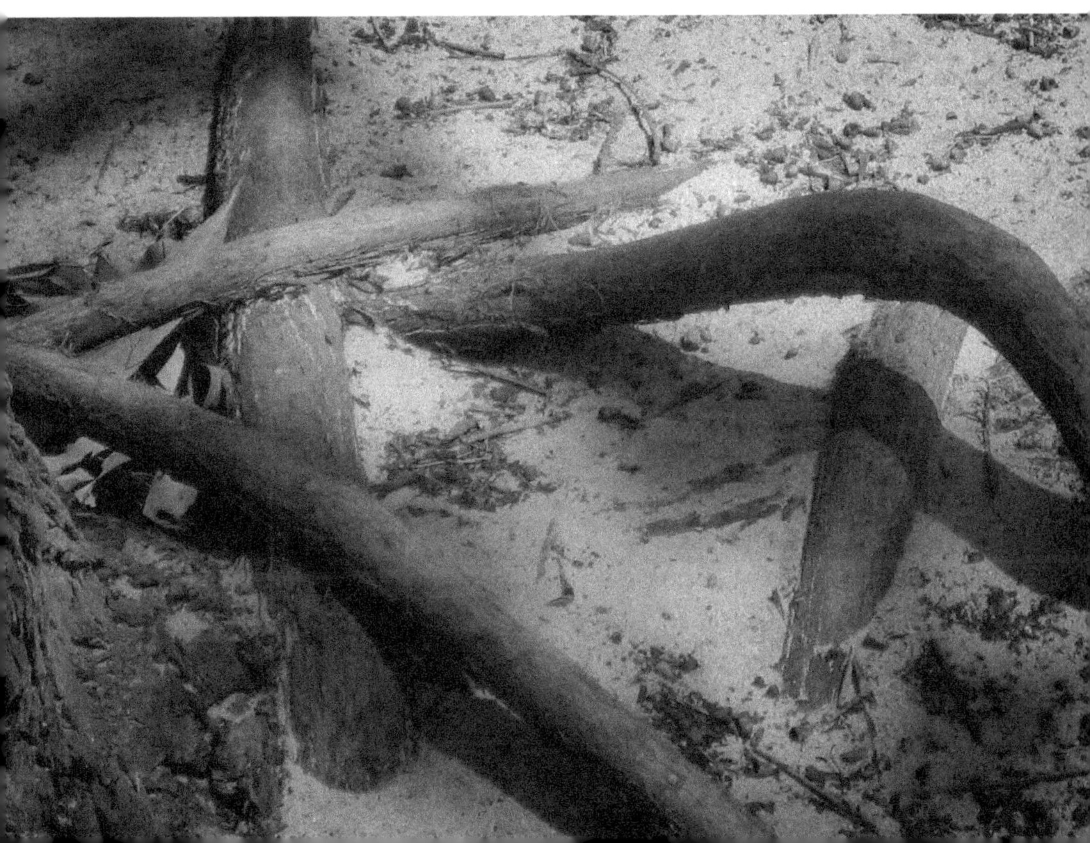

Breaking

i'm a loser
i'm pathetic
i pick women
who can't love me back
they don't want me

they don't want me
they want someone else
more attractive, smarter
less awkward, more sure
less fat

i'm emotionally safe
i will not harm
i feel i have no charm
certainly no confidence

warm and caring
emotional, sharing
empathic and understanding
just not head of hair
and sexy daring

oh to be wanted
oh to be desired
to be wanted for me

i hope it's something
that's about you
i fear it's me
and that something
i fear quite deep

i care, i love you
i hope you love me
and desire me in some way
as much, as i, you

i want love, i want care
i don't want to be hideous
a turn off, undesired
only okay since i can love

if that is it, then i can deal
the heart is pure and wants love true

i feel it deep
it know it true
but my pain knows fear
so. i. do. to.

fear is my burden
i know too well
please understand
it hurts me too

i want to be loved
i want it to be true
please love me deeply
please love me true

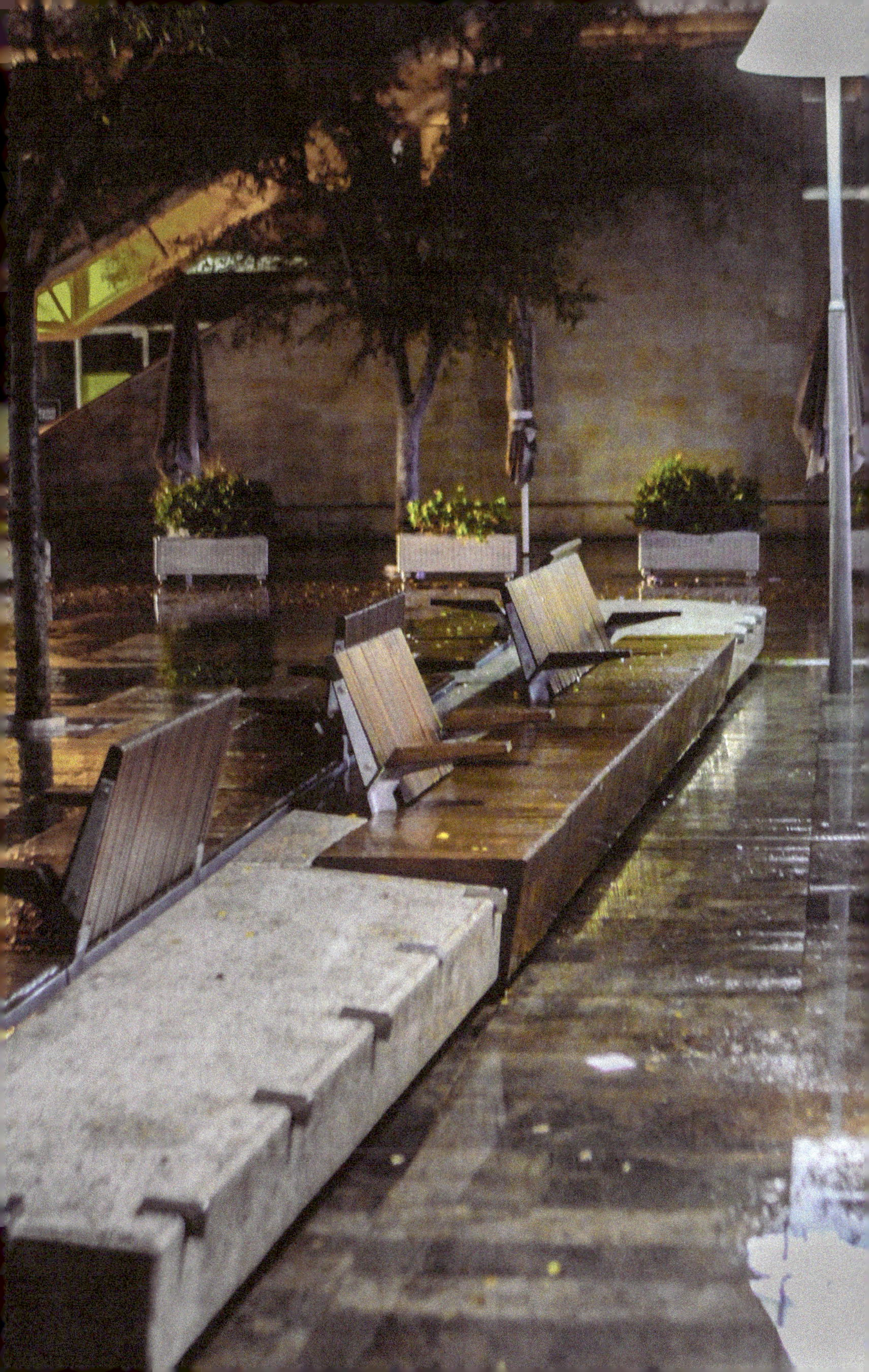

i felt the earth move
i quaked alone

in my sky bound view
i peered at you removed
a distant sight
a quiet picture

a scene from a movie
i yell and scream
no sound is coming
my tongue has been removed

if the wall was glass
i could smash through
i could speak
...connect with you

a bundle of words
my heart yearns to touch yours
they fail me now
i am alone

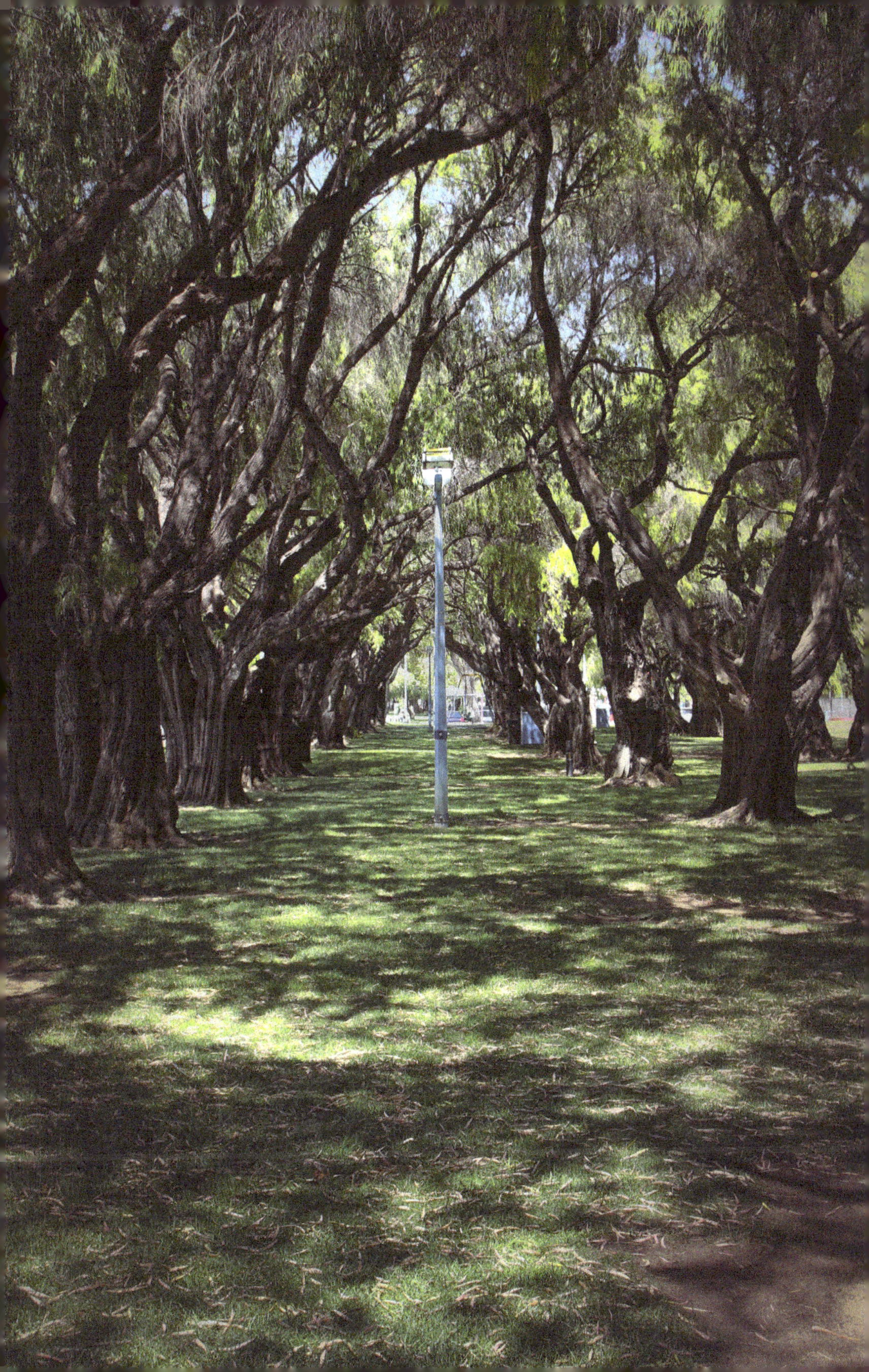

fear gripped my heart
one finger at a time
digging & clawing flesh

how could she do it
after so much care
i have given her

is my heart leather
booted with the foot and
sent away when play ends
...the day is done

could her heart be so cold
while her hands were so warm
i held her heart, and she mine
i thought, i knew her
so i let her inside

the pain, the hurt
my quiet destroyed
my heart, my life, my guts
ripped....trampled
callously laid aside

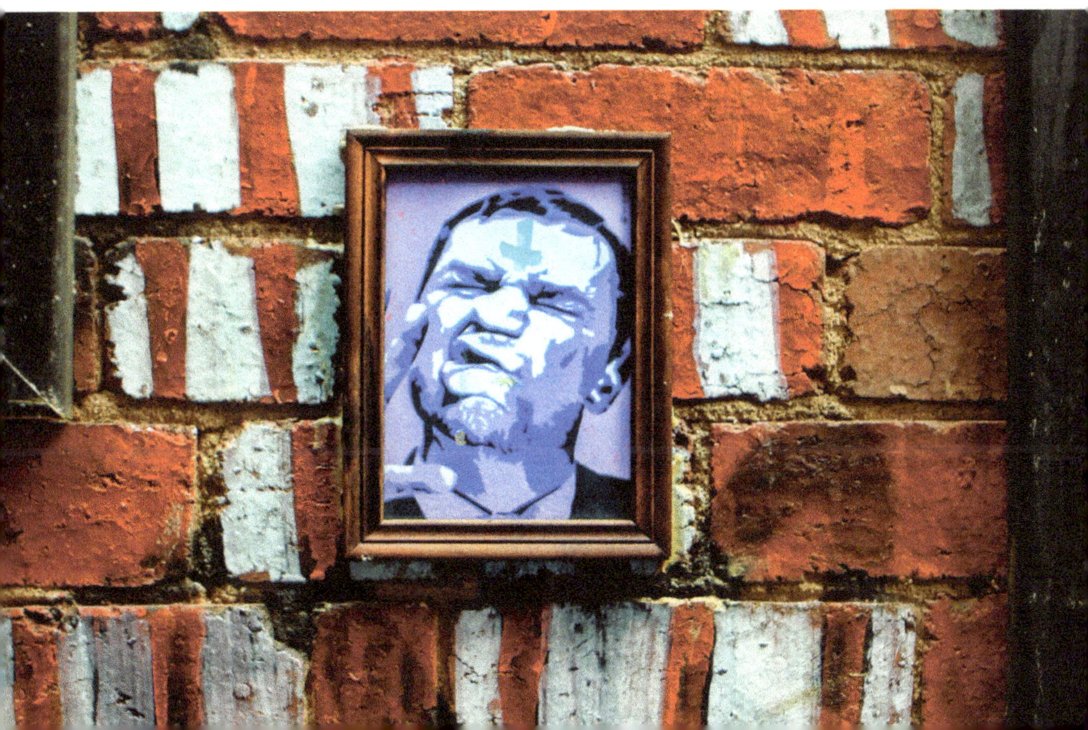

you tore my heart from my chest
ripped it out
one message at a time
i saw them
they scrolled past
my heart broke
my words lost
incredulous frozen mind
heart seared by fire

my safe place you were
when all else failed you were
my rock you were
my place of safety

yet you had stopped
i didn't know it
till i landed hard
broken on a tablet
words scrolling past

i knew you had gone
your place had drifted
we seldom connected
the bonds were weak
they were incomplete

when the msgs fell
no sense could be formed
the glue that bound was not enough
only shattered fragments remain

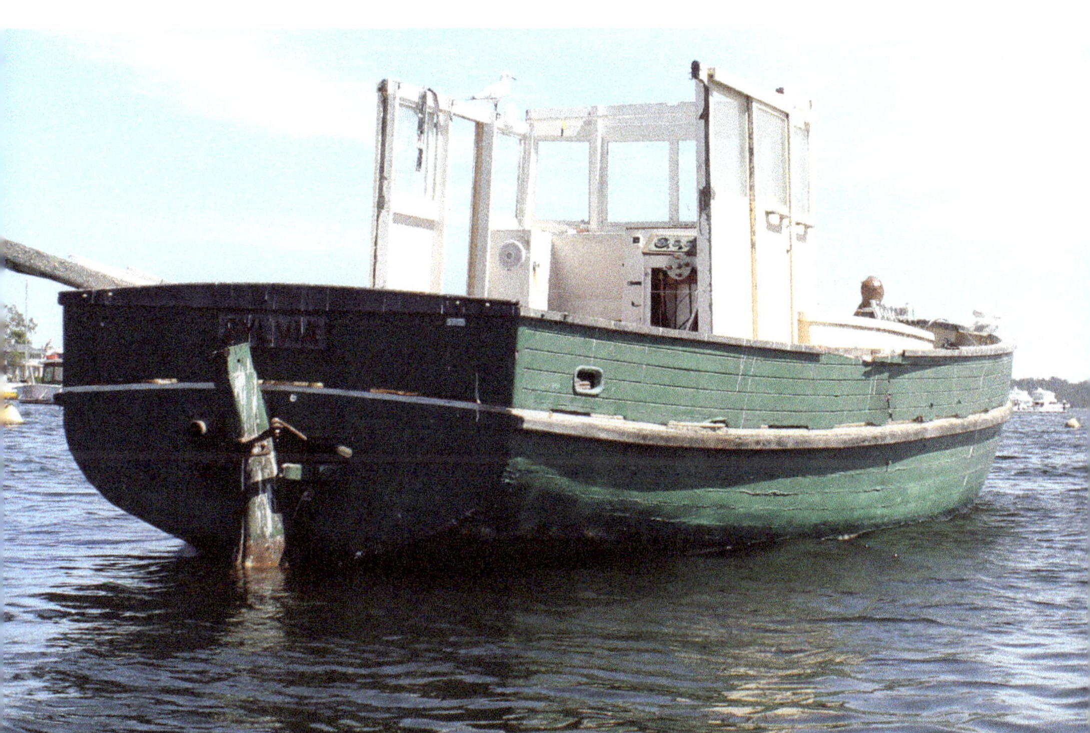

Leaving

so many lies
the vase has crumbled
i know no glue
that can hold
its powder

to hold its shape
with any meaning
structure is gone
material is crumble
it is dust
laying in the mantle

did it break at once
or was it made of
broken pieces

of course
it must have been
it could have been beautiful
now it is powder
now waste

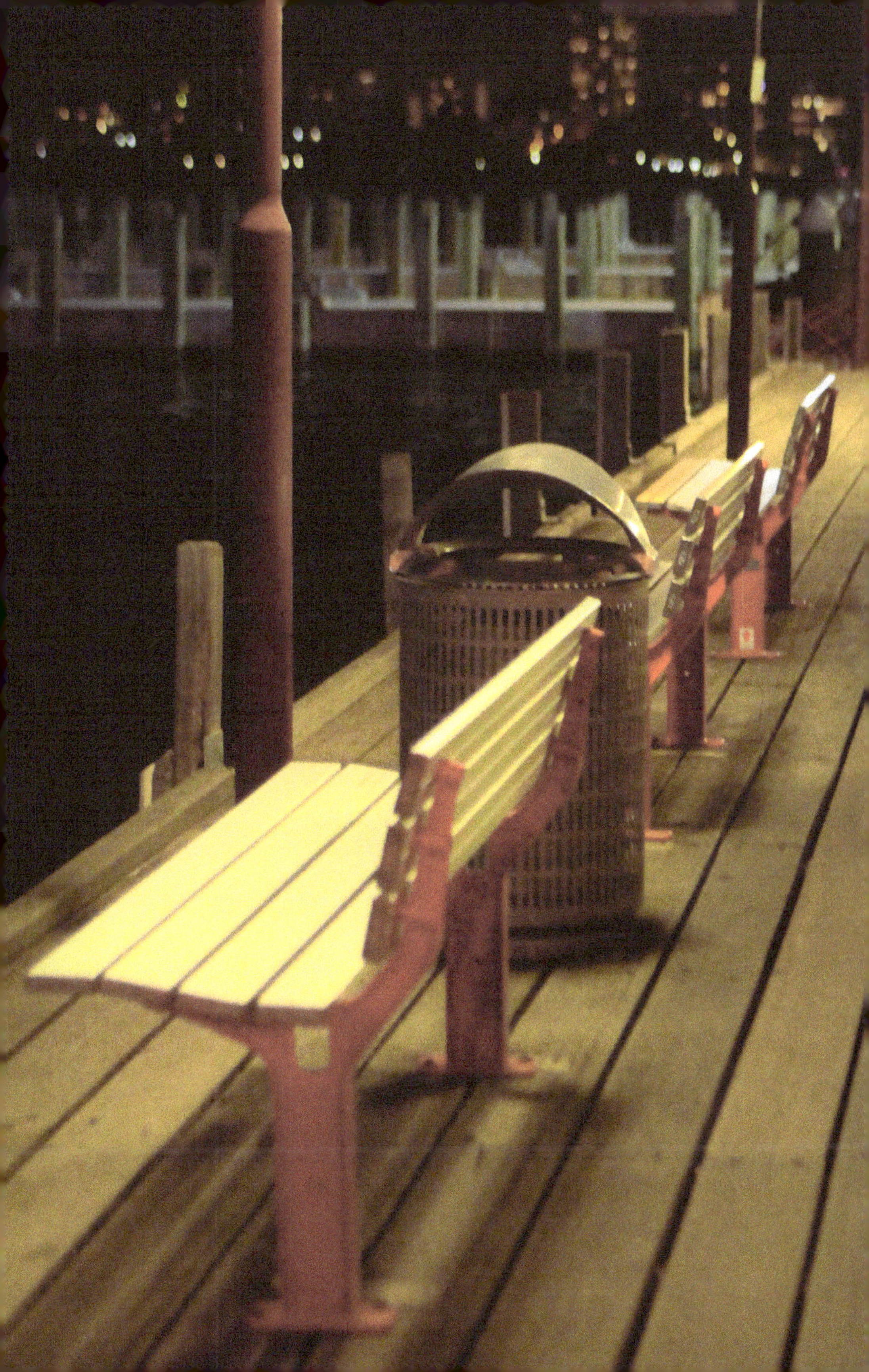

i loved you
did i not?
i'd have died
to see you live
i held you on a
pedestal so high
i dare not approach

yet you fell
so hard and so far
i didn't know
you who you were
when you landed below

i don't know what
to do to make it okay
up is now down
trust is...well??

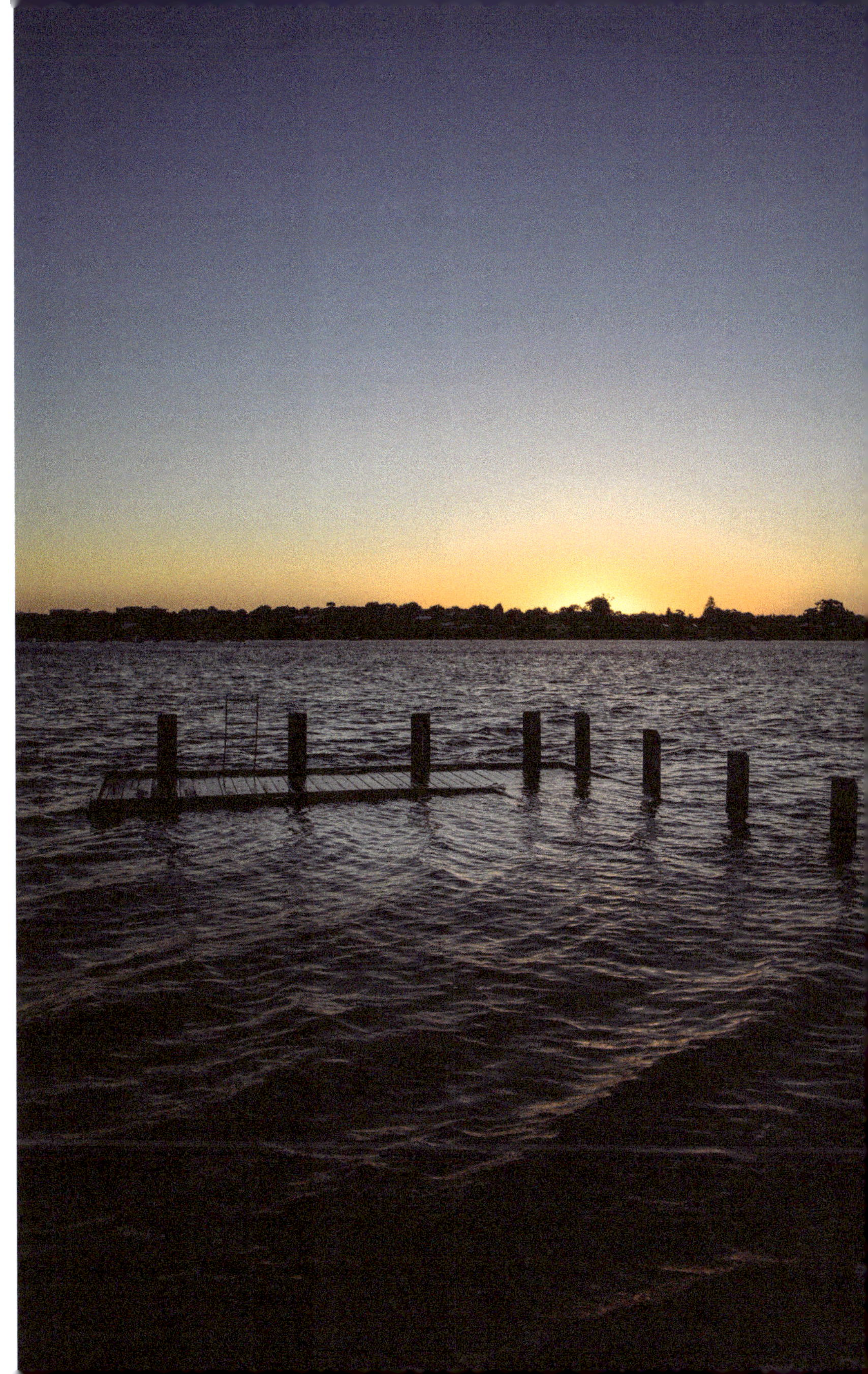

hope was WHAT?
was it in you
i dare not
was it coming back?
why try AGAIN?

twice burn't
thrice shy!
the heart has known
only one true love
it. is. not. you.

i thought you would
be the rock, in the storms
but the stone fish moved
i didn't know what to do
now i wander alone

well that's not true
it's just not with you

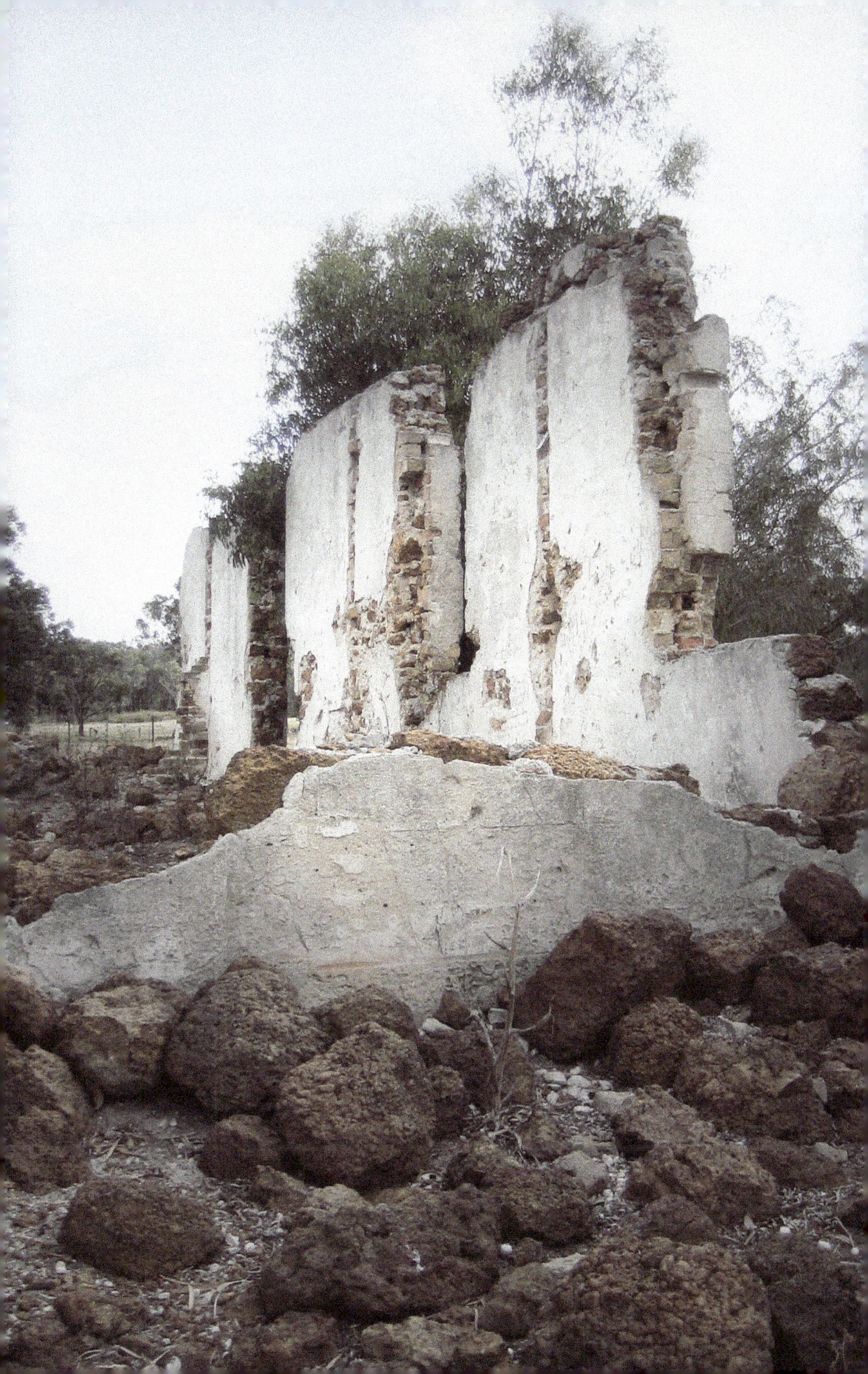

lonely, cold inside
responsible for me
responsible for none

i want heat, warmth
to feel safe
i want commitment
but it bares me

i want life
but it's full of fear

do i travel alone?
stand in my own cold

do i share my fire
with another?
and face the fear
they will flee too?

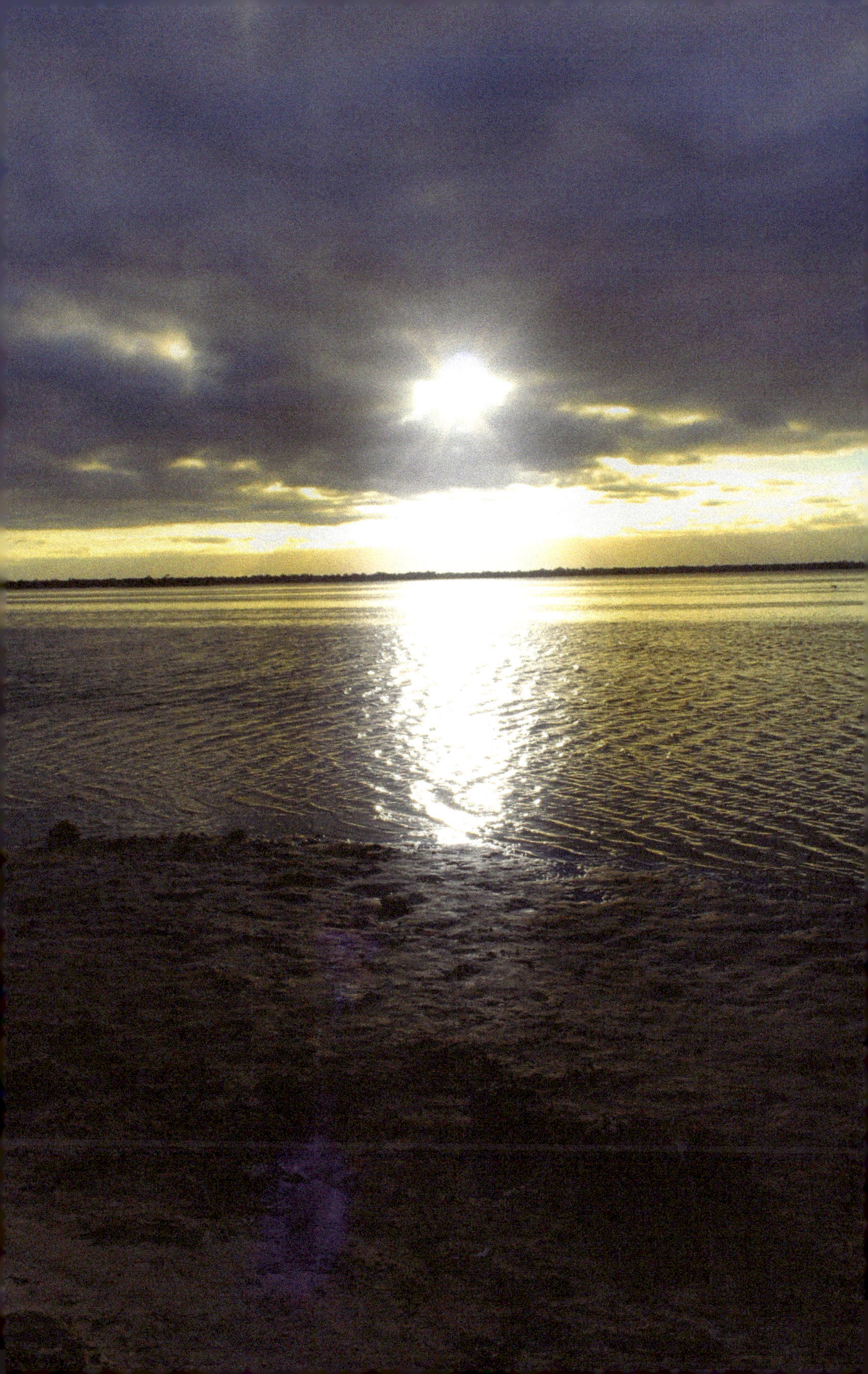

no more crying
no more alone
no more dark nights
no more pain
no more fearful unknown
no more yelling and hiding
no more being alone
no more hitting or hurting
no more words of spite
no more abusive sprouting of lies
no more outside cold of the night
no more closed doors and heartless crys

i will no more be thrust into night
nights of tears of pain and fear
no more threats of destruction
to what I hold tight

i will no more be a victim in the night

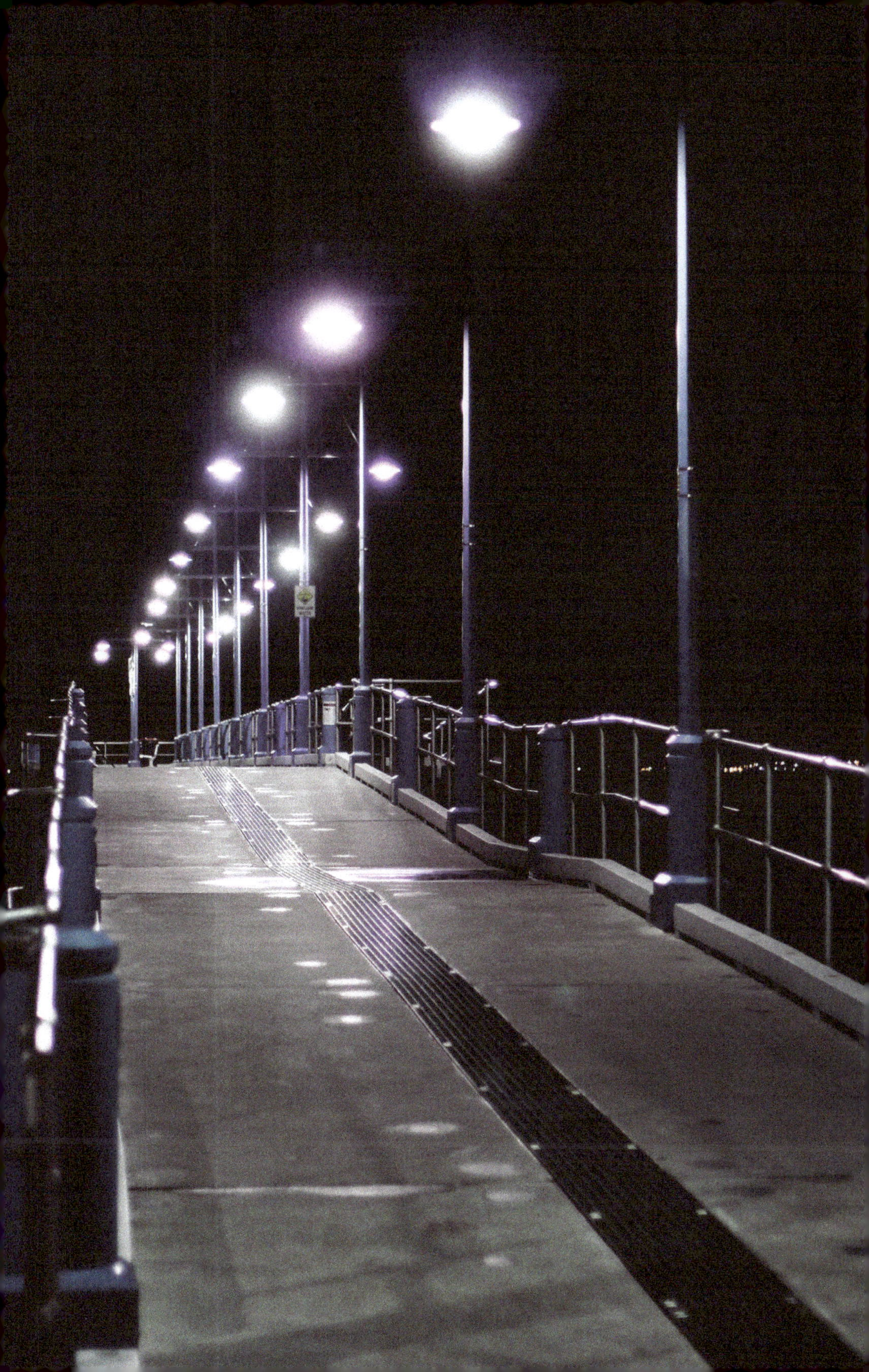

Hoping

i'm a mess
up is down
straight seems bent
life quaked
never the same

sad i am
hopeful too
pain will never be replaced
but sadness can fade
hope springs anew
companions abound
especially you

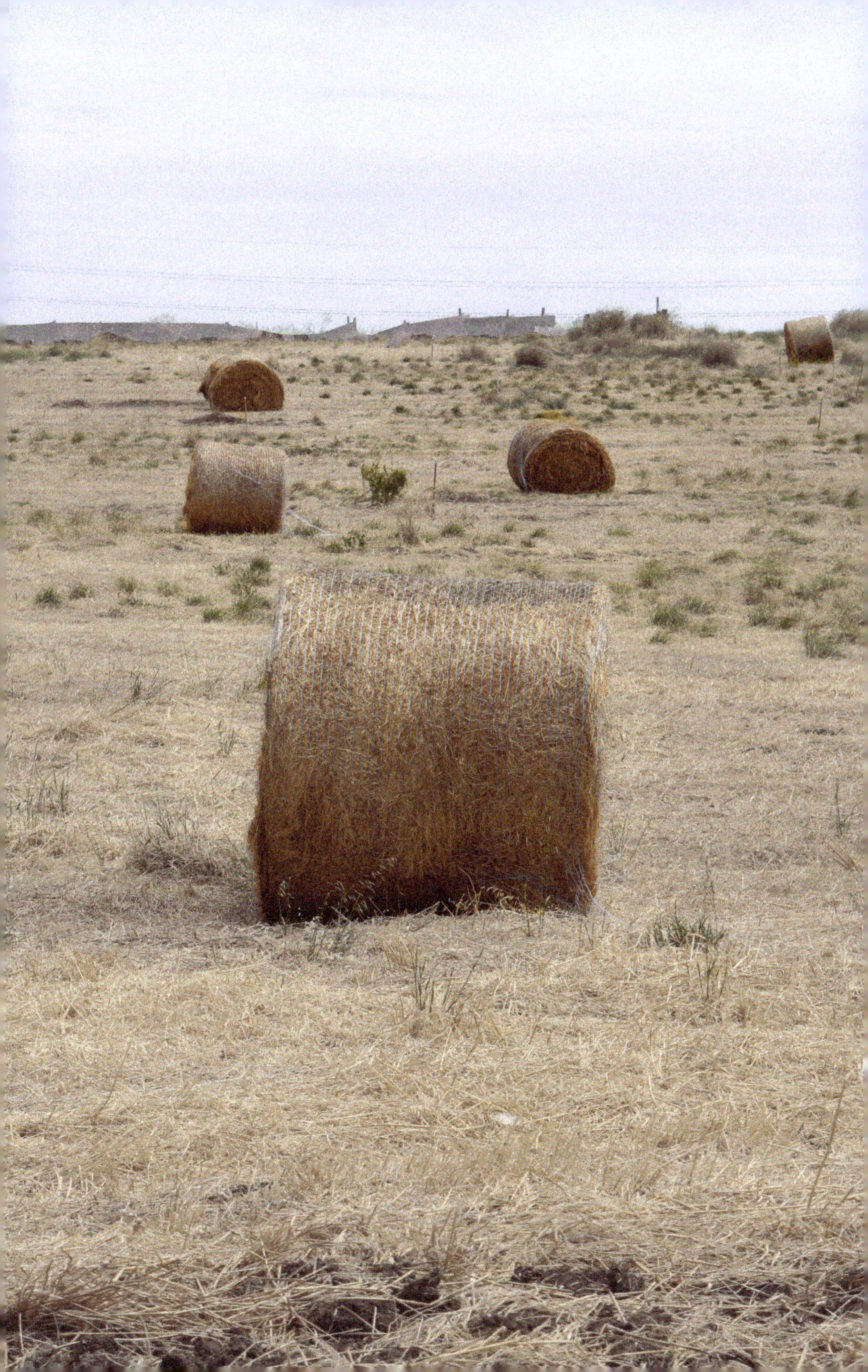

i miss the touch of a woman
the gentle sweet caress
firm but gentle yearning
for the tight embrace

i want to be held
to find my meaning there
then lose myself
in her heart and
in her hair

to her beauty i will yield
in her stare i will dare
to find more meaning
than my heart can bare

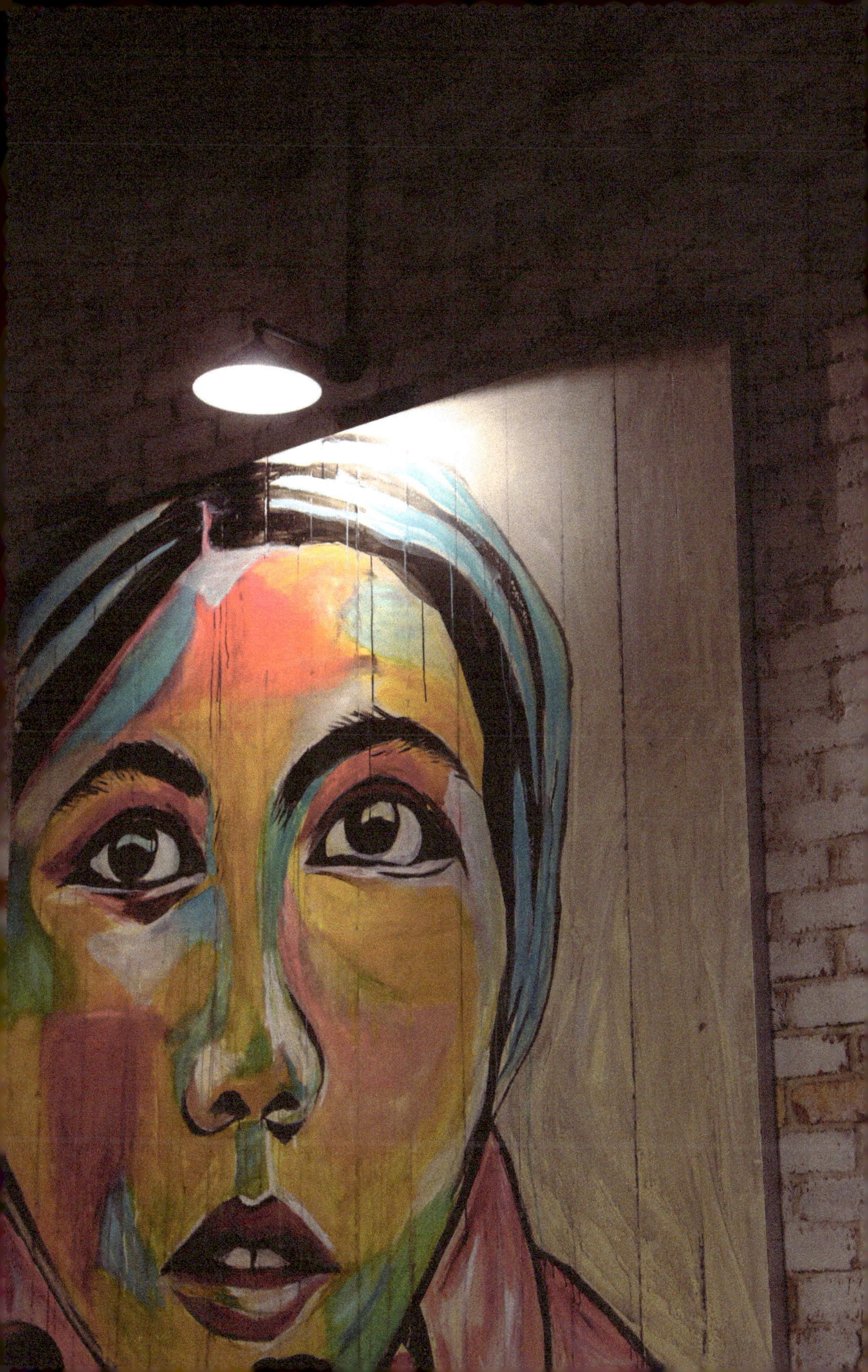

feelings inside i cannot hide
welling within, an emotional tide
a surge, some spray
what a way to begin the day

a heartbeat longer
a heartbeat stronger
one more chance to tempt my fate

love me yes, emotions unknown
what a way to spend a day
limbo and float
will she
or
won't

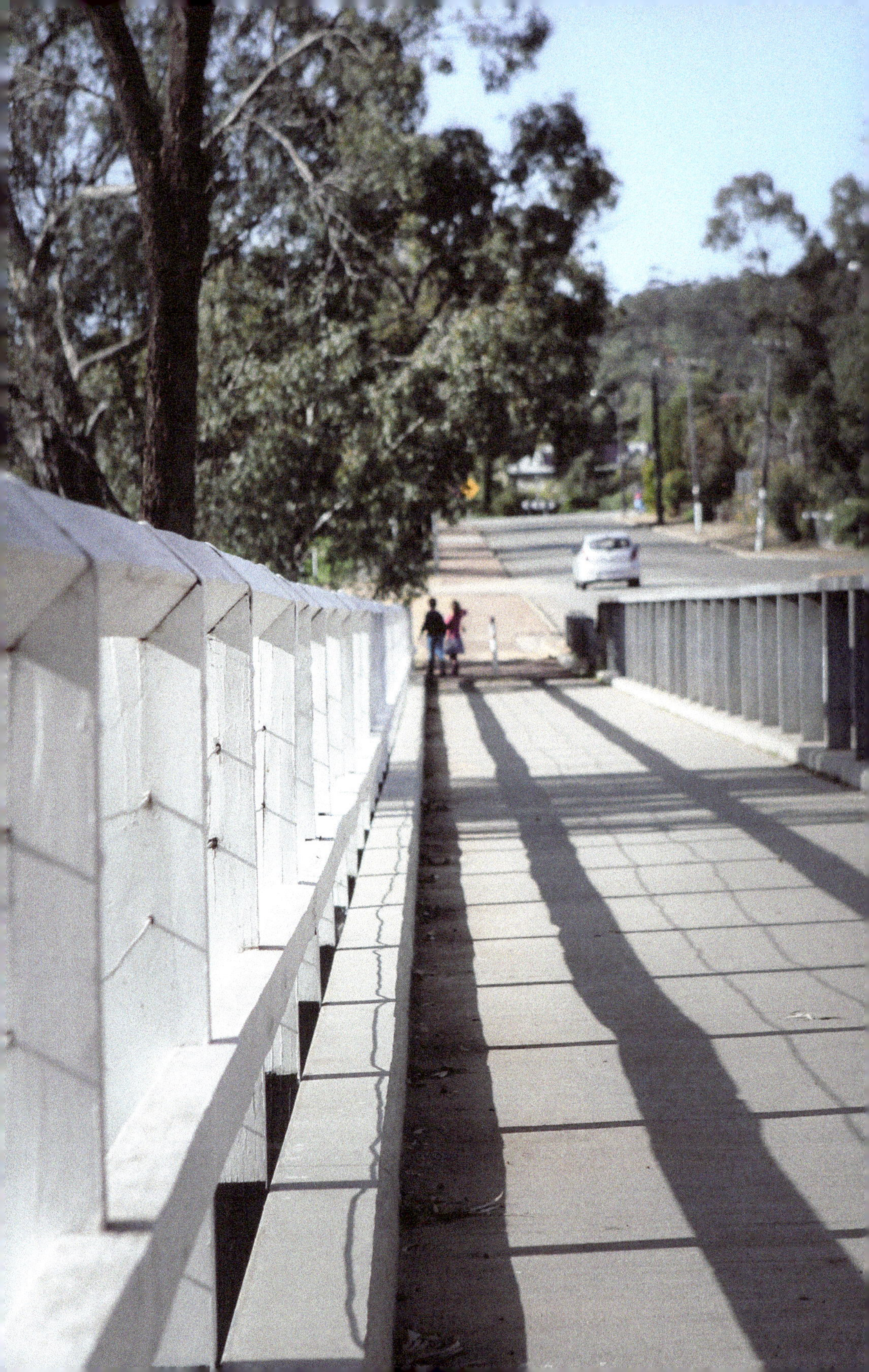

i'm in a rush
she makes me blush
proud and ashamed
i'm her man but i'm not the same

i want to be her man
to make her proud
for me to feel the same

i'm learning to trust
to settle from the rush
to let it build
learning to trust

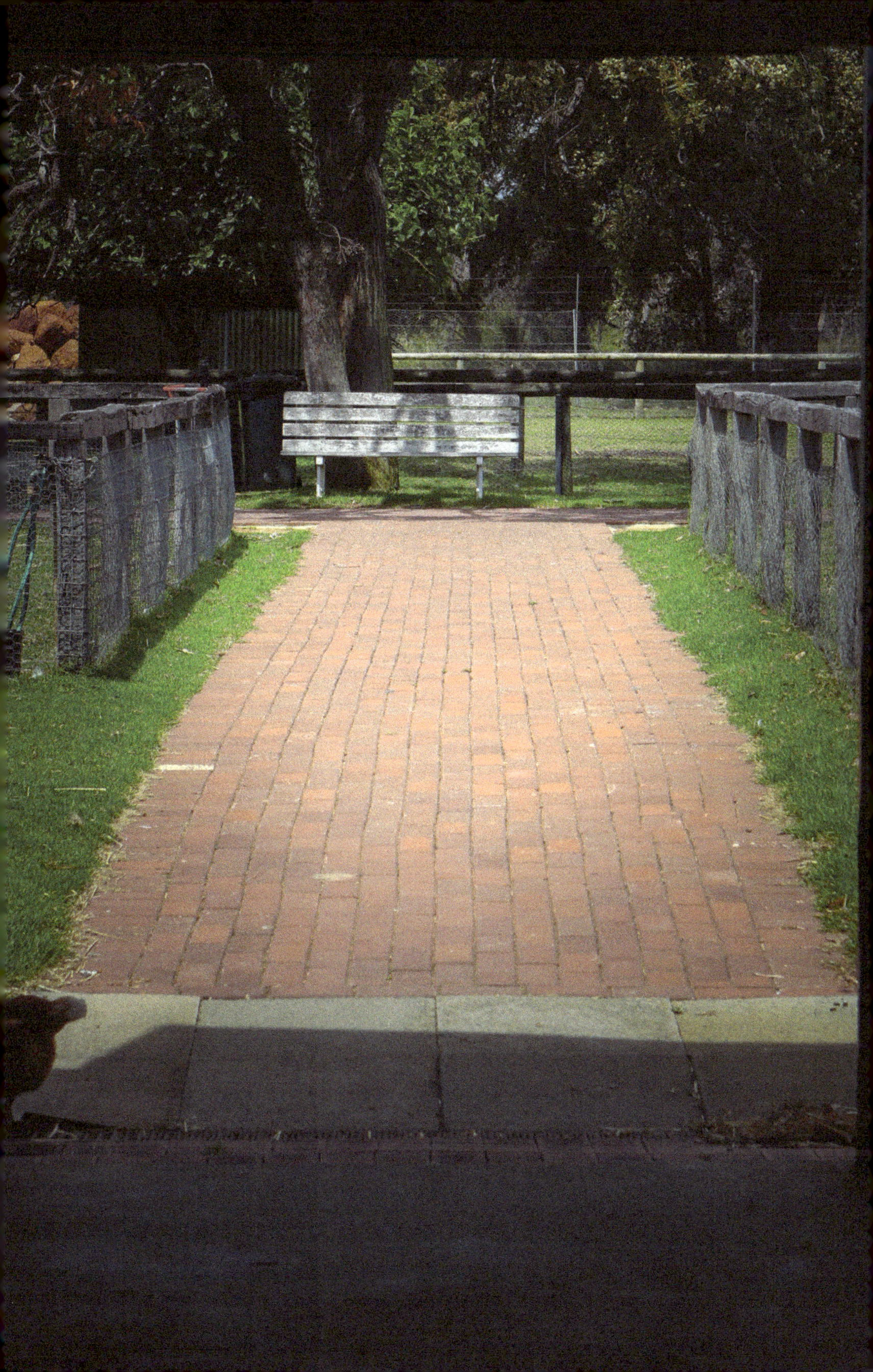

the dance continues
partners change
steps alter
their moods range

rhythm slows
hearts beat longer
my heart beats stronger

passion wells within
my heart is alive
my passion has fire
desire flows, yearning grows

my dear one
sweetly innocent, deeply aware
dangerously calm, elegantly composed
moved by emotion, moved by mine

your heart's my friend
let's journey to places we've never known
let's hold hands
let's hold hearts
let's share lives

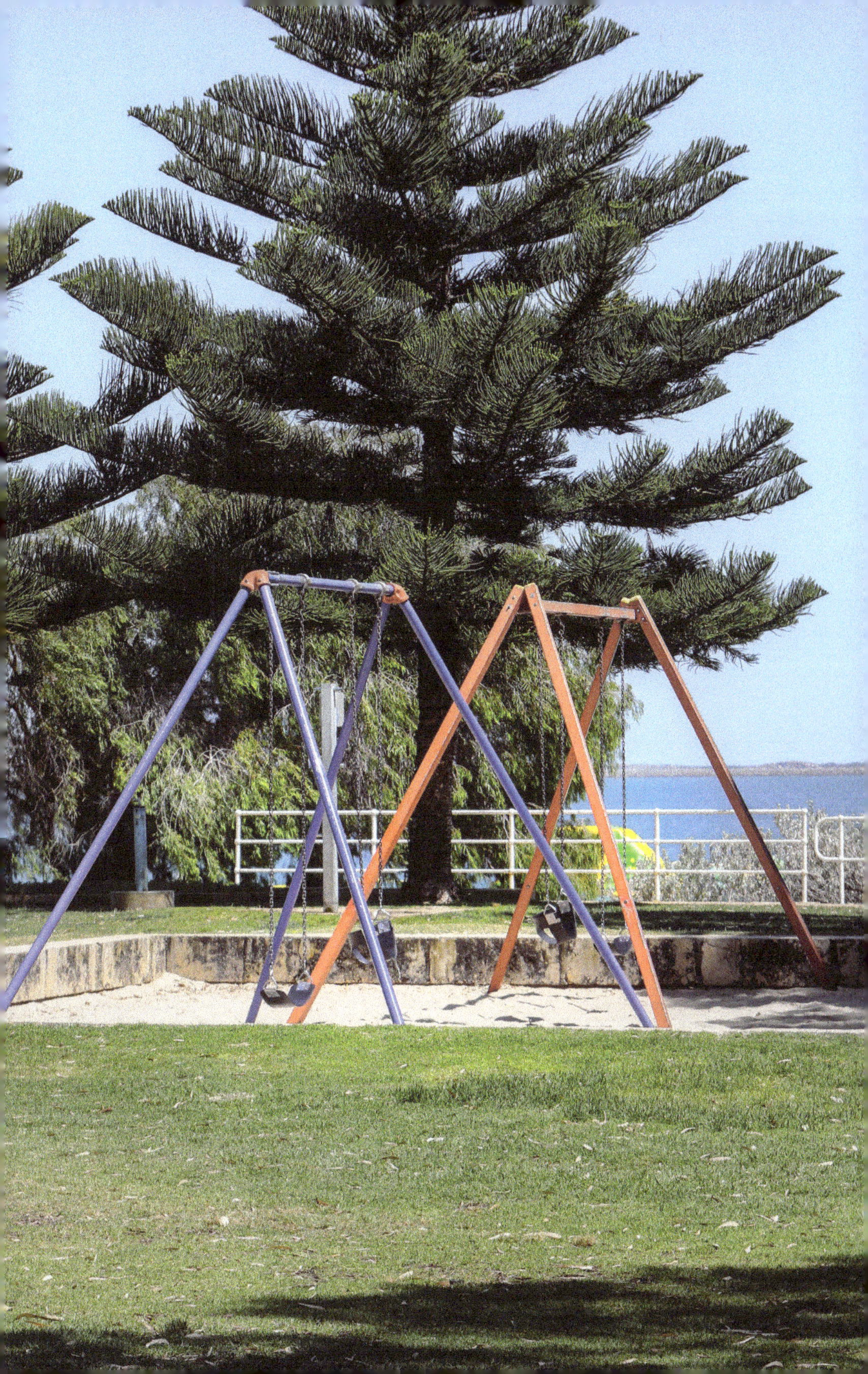

www.ingramcontent.com/pod-product-compliance
Ingram Content Group UK Ltd.
Pitfield, Milton Keynes, MK11 3LW, UK
UKHW062301290726
14090UKWH00017B/815